# STATUESQUE BUFFALO

**Secrets about our amazing city as told**

**by our monuments, landmarks and public art**

photography and writing by

Mark D. Donnelly, Ph.D.

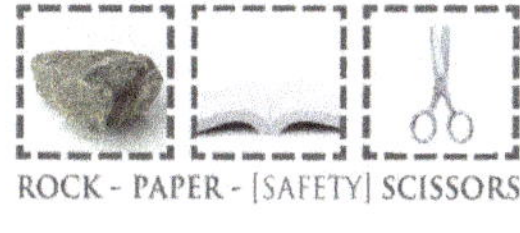

ROCK - PAPER - [SAFETY] SCISSORS

**BUFFALO, NEW YORK**

Permissions, Rock Paper [Safety] Scissors Publishing, 2495 Main Street, Suite 429a, Buffalo, NY 14214

www.rockpapersafetyscissors.com

Writing, photography, and design by Mark D. Donnelly, Ph.D.

ISBN 978-0-9848787-4-1

Printed in the United States of America

10 9 8 7 6 5 4 3 2 1

We live in a city overflowing with wonder.
Stop and smell the sculpture.

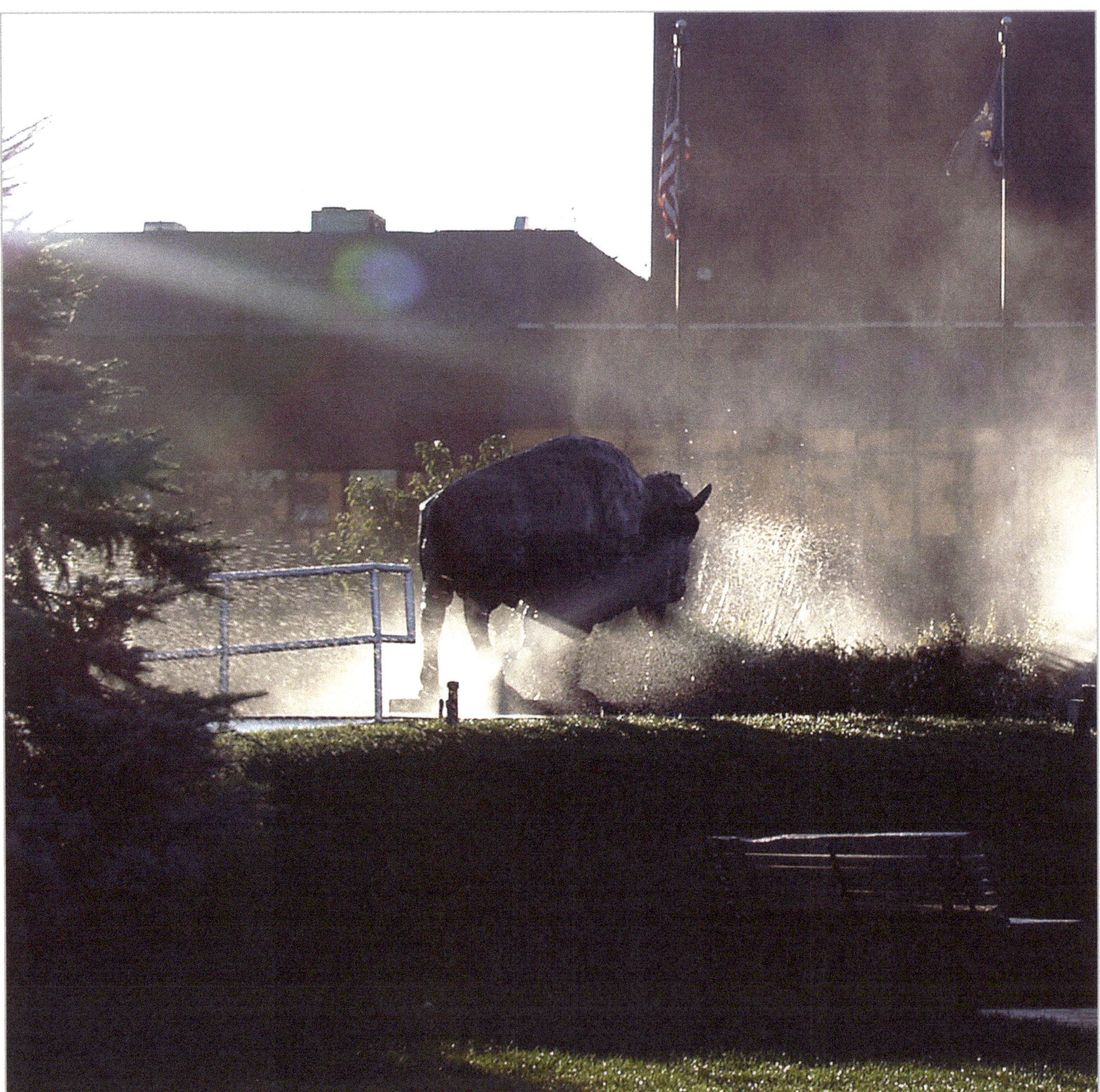

# Table of Contents



## Smelly when wet

*(left and front cover)*

Wandering in the academic wilderness of the University at Buffalo's North Campus, this flightless mammal, tragically known best for the wings it wish it had, takes the time on summer mornings for a pre-class run through the sprinkler.

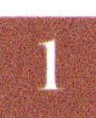

**University at Buffalo, North Campus**
103 Center For The Arts, Buffalo, NY 14260

# Introduction

I stand here atop my soapbox to brag about our monuments, landmarks, and public art, and to use them to anecdotally connect the history that binds our collective narrative as a region.

At first blush, it's easy to view the dozens of monuments that dot our landscape as merely bronze mannequins that glorify war or bolster the empty vanities of dead politicians. Or to look at our sculpture as "plop," the pejorative slang term for public art, connoting work that is inappropriate to its surroundings, as though it were thoughtlessly "plopped" there like municipal lawn furniture.

As the city internationally known for banishing a sculpture featuring dancing neon genitalia, Buffalo has admittedly accumulated its fair share of stone and metal offenders. Fortunately, these are by far and away the exceptions rather than the rule. On closer inspection, we have amassed an embarrassment of cultural and historic riches that connect us to our local past like an intricate work of string art.

In my semi-conflicted role as both an amateur history wonk and an artist, I've developed an unusual habit. I actually stop and read the plaques that accompany each statue. Then I often find myself doing a bit of research to help put it in context. Over the years I've concluded that these works go well beyond simply memorializing or adding a splash of random color. They actually stand vigil, serving as time machines and silent sentinels in our neighborhoods.

**36**

**"The Hiker" by Allen George Newman**
- Roosevelt Plaza - Main Street at Huron, Buffalo, NY, 14202
- Pine Avenue at Portage Street, Niagara Falls, NY 14301

These works of art have  nothing but time on their hands to listen and observe, and they have volumes to share if we take a moment to listen.

Our public art and statues are steadfast witnesses to our past, as well as being slices of  history in their own right. Even though they are technically lifeless, they have the ability to project a feeling beyond the moment, beyond our lifetimes, and as close to forever as humans are capable of stealing from the weather and oxidation.

All too often these cultural custodians, despite their enormous size, hide in plain sight, becoming such a predictable part of our local tapestry that they are virtually invisible. We whisk by them in our cars at dizzying speeds, or we walk, on, over and around them without even noticing them. I often joke that our military would be miles ahead if they designed our stealth weapons to look like Spanish-American War monuments.

I sincerely hope that this book can help bend perceptions and begin to open our eyes to the countless treasures that surround us. And even though real historians define anecdotal history like this as "probably wrong," I hope you enjoy these stories, compiled to amplify our connections to the past.

## Jungle-inspired fashion-plate

With his hand on his hip, sporting a wide-brimmed hat tipped to one side, an open-necked shirt, laced leggings, and a retro ammo belt, this Spanish-American War fashionista is sure to be the hit of this Fall's runway.

There are more than 75 castings  of "The Hiker" scattered all over the country - two in Western New York alone. Because of the wide distribution of these statues, they have recently been used to study air pollution over the last century.

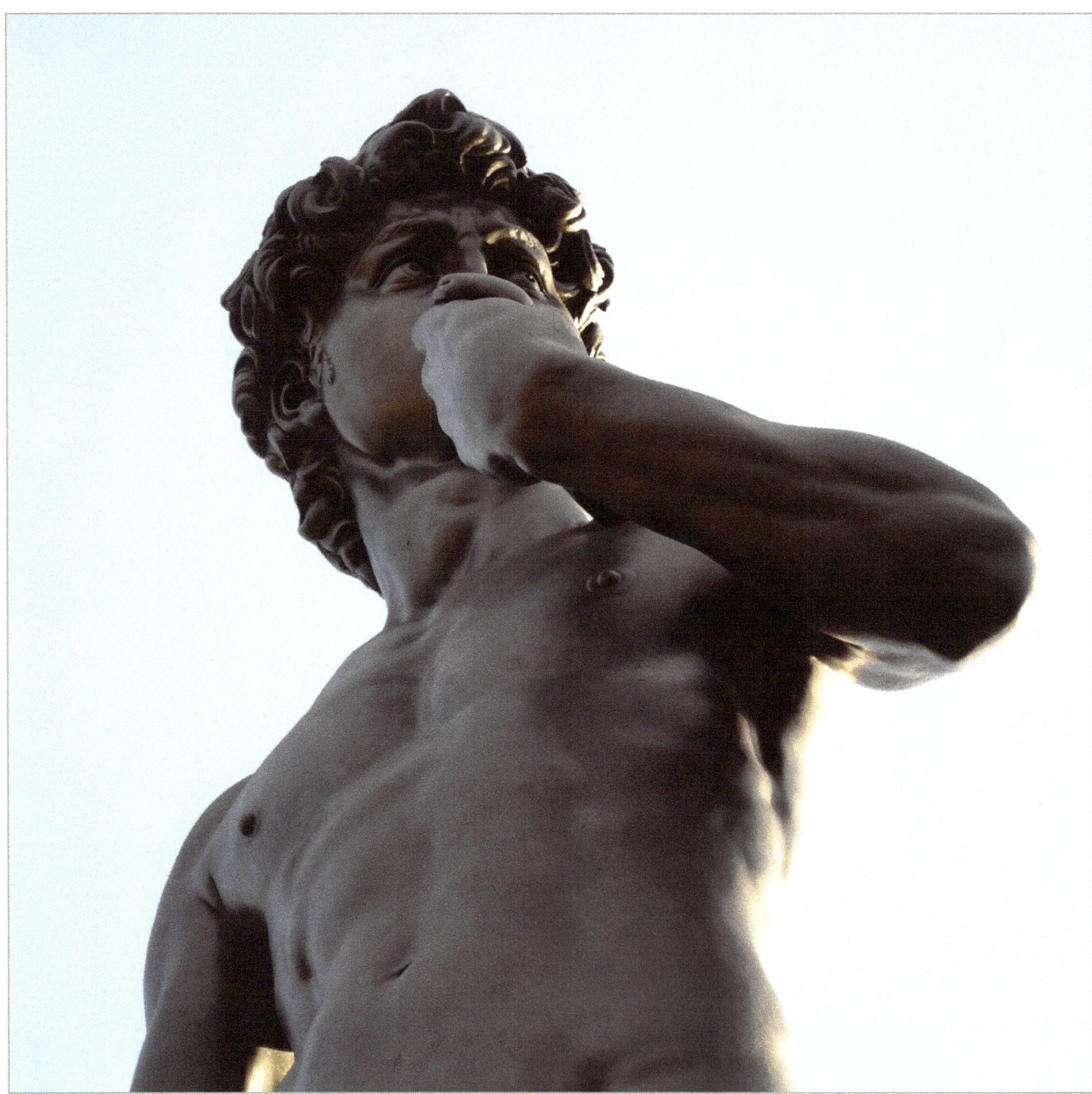

# Woman raped by statue of David

Allow me to re-create the crime scene. It was the spring of 1981 in Delaware Park, in a then wooded section between Hoyt Lake and the Scajaquada expressway. A muscular young man stood perched on a large slab of marble, as naked as the day he was born. He had a weapon powerful enough to take down a giant slung over his shoulder and three pieces of ammunition in his hand. One of a long string of rapes took place here, but this man was not the villain; he was merely a silent witness.

Had the classical statue of Michelangelo's David been able to speak, he may have prevented the wrongful conviction of an innocent man and been able to reveal the true identity of a serial rapist who terrorizeded the women of Western New York for decades.

Anthony J. Capozzi, the man who was wrongfully incarcerated following his 1985 arrest for two Buffalo rapes, spent more than 20 years of his 35-year sentence in state prison.  He was exonerated in 2007 using DNA evidence which had been taken from two Delaware Park sex attack victims but was misplaced in a drawer at the Erie County Medical Center (ECMC) for more than 20 years. The DNA positively linked the "bike path rapist" and murderer Altemio Sanchez to these crimes.

The statue of the Biblical hero David is a copy of Michelangelo's masterpiece, which stands in the Piazzetta Michelangelo in Florence, Italy. The bronze replica was purchased at the Paris Exposition in 1900 and gifted to the City of Buffalo Historical Society by Andrew Langdon.

**5**

**"David," by Michaelangelo Burnarroti** (replica)
Delaware Park, near Scajaquada Expressway, Buffalo, NY 14216

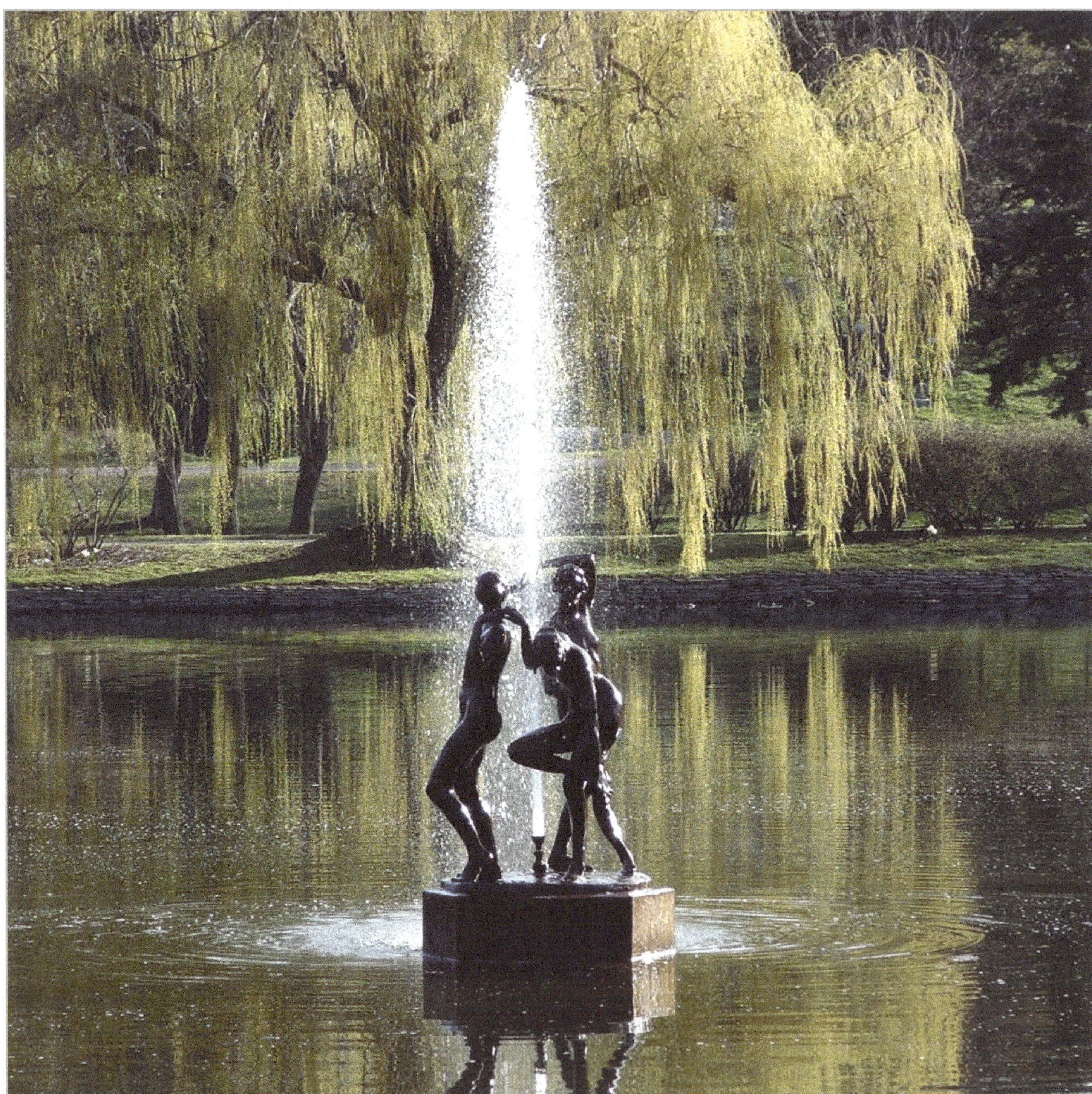

# Skinny-dipping in Mirror Lake

Where in Buffalo can you go for a clothing-optional splash?

For more than 25 years, three women – Aglaia, Eurphersyne and ThaIia – have been witnessed taking a spritely frolic in a fountain right smack in the geographic center of the city. Wearing nothing but their smiles, these women are constantly surrounded by hundreds, who so far have kept quiet about their escapades, but are dying to tell.

"The Three Graces" fountain sculpture by Buffalo-born Charles Cary Rumsey (1879–1922) is located on Mirror Lake in Forest Lawn Cemetery. Originally designed for railroad magnate Edward H. Harriman, a recast was donated in 1987 by the Rumsey and Goodyear families.

Rumsey was commissioned to create a series of sculptures to decorate the Harriman's estate on the Hudson River in 1909. Edward's daughter Mary Harriman was said to have modeled for some of his sculptures. They were married in 1910.

The cemetery serves as one the world's finest outdoor museums. Among its monuments, sculptures, and mausoleums are many designed by great sculptors and architects, including Stanford White, Augustus Saint-Gaudens, E.B. Green, Richard Upjohn, N. Cantalamessa-Papotti, George Cary, and Frank Lloyd Wright.

4

**"The Three Graces," by Charles Cary Rumsey**
Forest Lawn Cemetery - Mirror Lake
1411 Delaware Avenue, Buffalo, NY 14209

# Up a tree without a paddle

If sculpture could talk, Los Angeles artist Nancy Rubins' bombastic new addition to the Albright-Knox Art Gallery front lawn would be screaming at the top of its lungs.

Seeming to defy all known laws of gravity, the 60-foot-tall piece resembling an explosion of dozens of shiny aluminum canoes has ignited a new energy on the historically safe and stoic gallery grounds. The 55 boats chaotically suspended in the air by stainless steel cable like a floral burst is a jarring counterpoint to the minimalist black, diamond-shaped sculpture by Antoni Milkowski it replaced.

Officially unveiled on June 30, 2011, the sculpture, whose equally ostentatious formal name is *Stainless Steel, Aluminum, Monochrome I, Built to Live Anywhere, at Home Here*, marks an obvious new trajectory for the gallery. It boldly challenges complacency, demanding that viewers walk out of their way to wander around and under it. It engages and expands the artistic presence of the gallery beyond the interior walls in much the way events like Rock'n at the Knox, Art Alive, and Music is Art have done.

**3**

**"Stainless Steel, Aluminum, Monochrome I," by Nancy Rubins**
Albright-Knox Art Gallery
1400 Elmwood Avenue, Buffalo, NY 14214

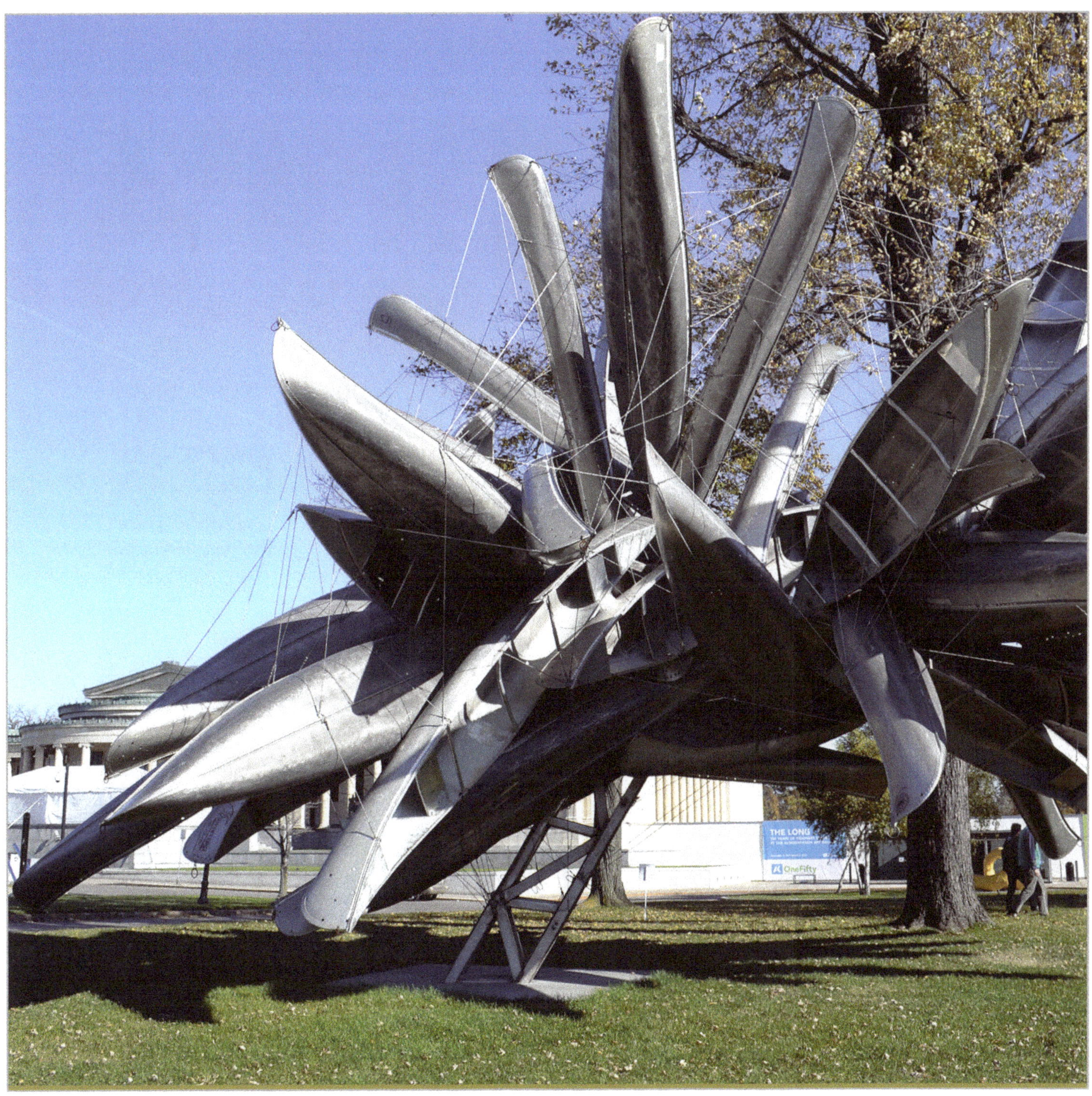

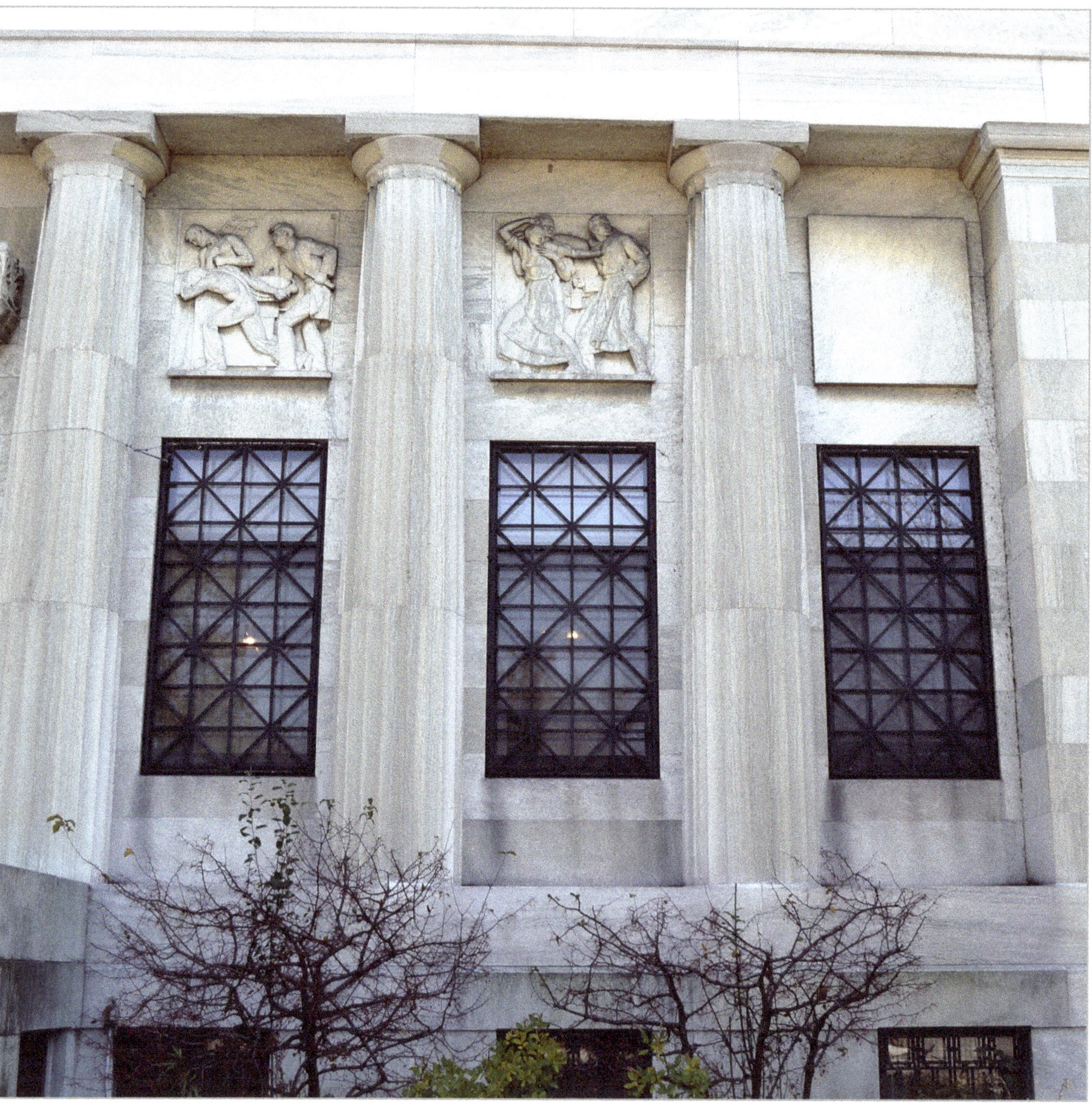

# One of these things is not like the others

Originally erected as the New York State Pavilion for the Pan-American Exposition of 1901, the The Buffalo History Museum building is the sole surviving permanent structure from this momentous event. The masterwork of Buffalo architect George Cary, the building's south portico is meant to evoke the Parthenon in Athens.

Edmund R. Amateis carved the series of relief sculptures that surround the building. These friezes depict scenes from Western New York history, such as the trial of Red Jacket, Commodore Perry at the Battle of Lake Erie, the burning of Buffalo, and the Underground Railway.

Amateis created eleven sculptures in all, but there were actually spaces provided for twelve. The great unsolved mystery is what happened to the twelfth sculpture. After considerable research, the sole explanation found is that only eleven sculptures were commissioned, curiously leaving a glaring blank space.

Human nature dictates that a vacuum like this would be filled by wild speculation. Some claim that this empty white space is reserved for when the Bills win the Super Bowl, or that it is really a view of the Skyway from the Blizzard of '77.

Personally, I like to think of it as a portal to the soul of our city projecting a bright and prosperous future.

**2**

**Relief Sculptures, by Edmund R. Amateis**
The Buffalo History Museum
One Museum Court, Buffalo, NY 14216

# The elephant in the room

Founded in 1875, the Buffalo Zoological Gardens is the third oldest zoo in the United States. The Zoo held 270 animals at the time of the Pan-American Exposition in 1901, including Big Frank, a 2,000 pound Asian elephant born in the wild in 1894. He was donated by his namesake, Buffalo lumber magnate Frank H. Goodyear, and arrived in October of 1900.

Big Frank was kept tethered outside year-round until a permanent elephant house, designed by noted local architects Esenwein and Johnson, was built in 1912.

Cantankerous and mischievous, yet very loved, Big Frank died in 1939. His likeness lives on through a high-relief sculpture of his head by Ira Lake which graces the entrance to the Elephant House.

An elephant named Koko, presented by Ismailia Shriners, continued the tradition of Big Frank in drawing big crowds.

Located on 23.5 acres of Olmsted's beautiful Delaware Park, the Buffalo Zoo today houses more than 1,200 endangered and domestic animals and offers visitors a variety of events and educational programs year-round. It welcomes more than 400,000 visitors each year, making it the most visited cultural attraction in Erie County.

6

**"Big Frank," by Ira Lake**
Buffalo Zoological Gardens - Elephant House
300 Parkside Avenue, Buffalo, NY 14214

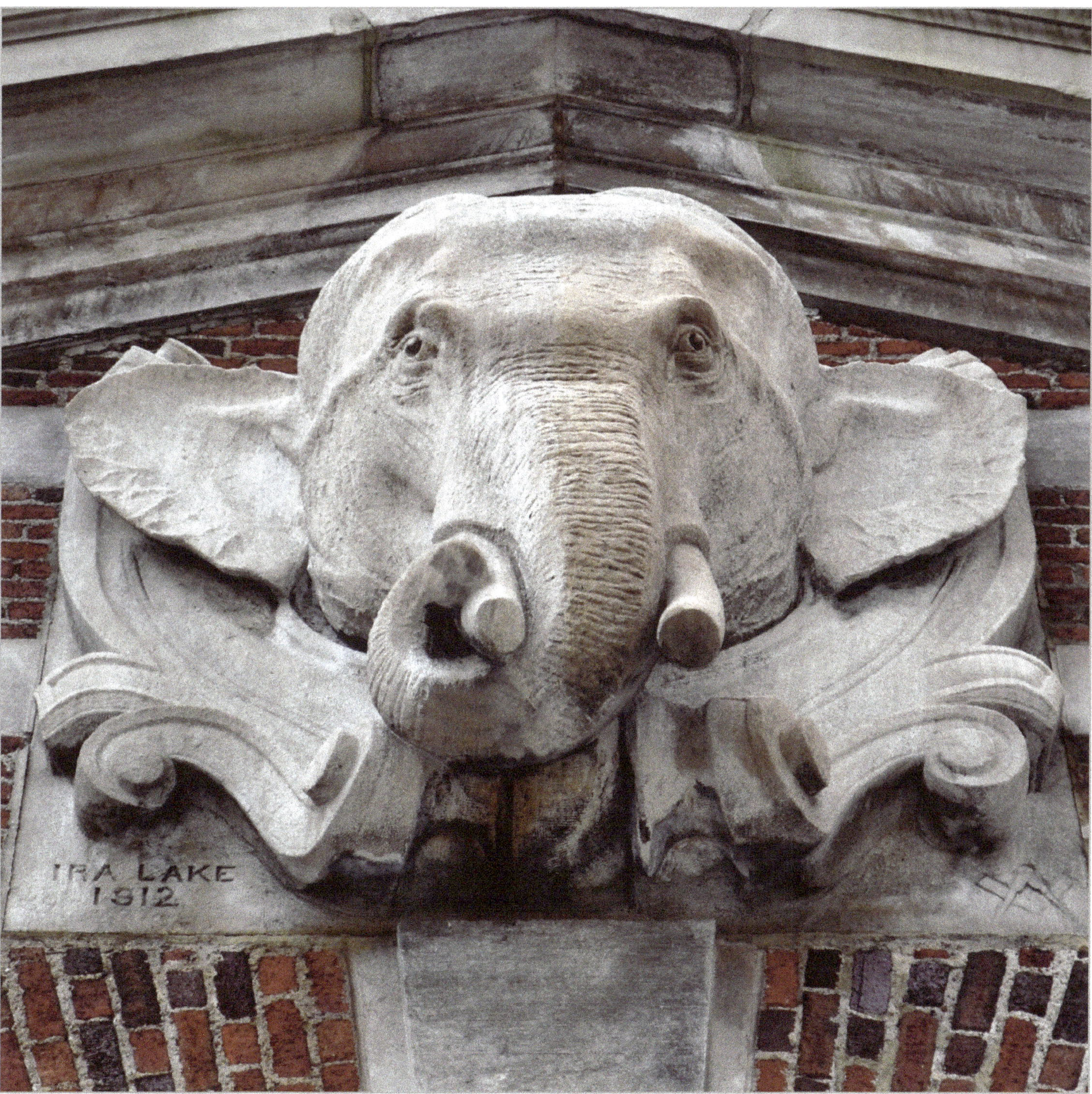


IRA LAKE
1912

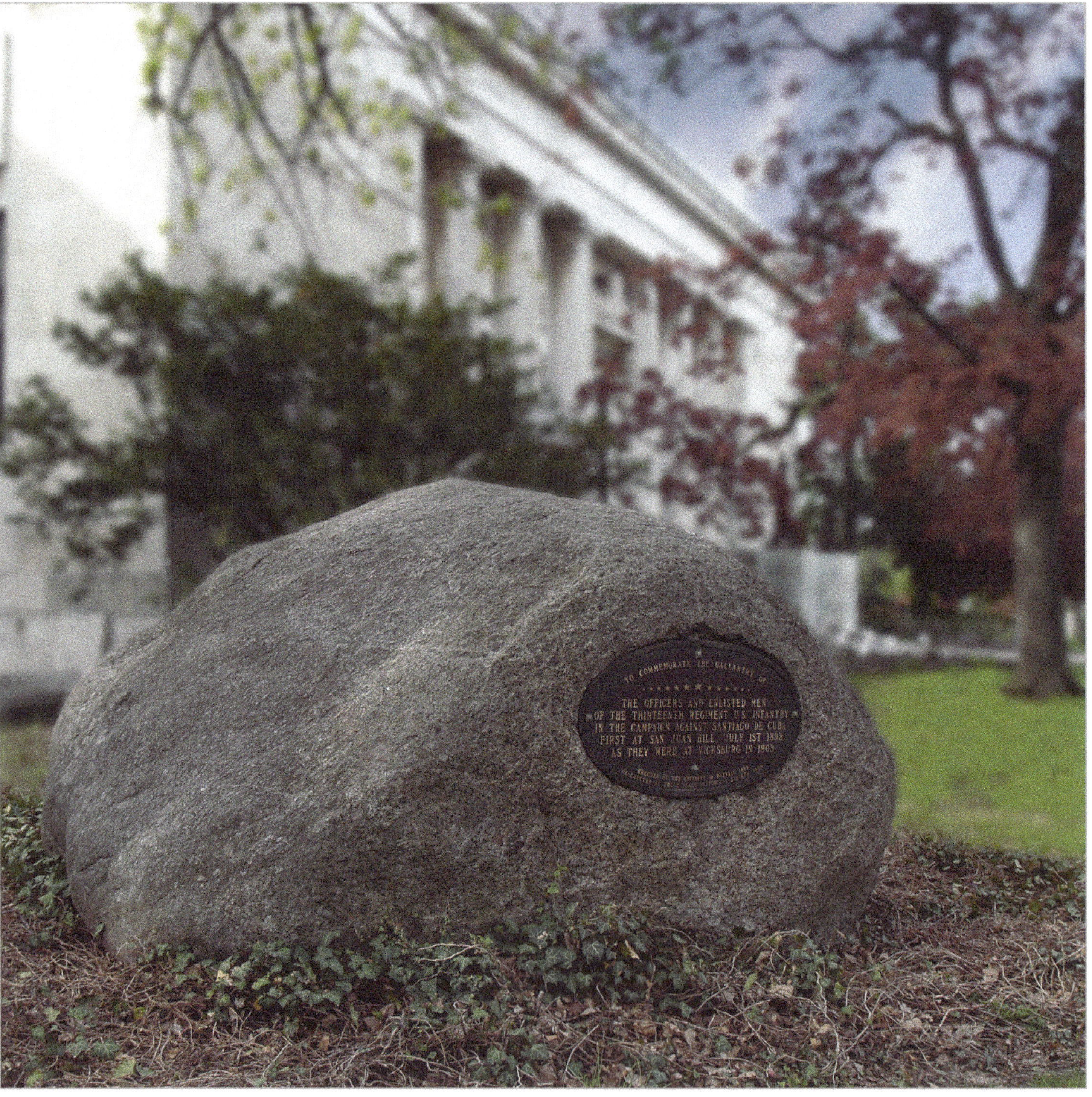
TO COMMEMORATE THE GALLANTRY OF
THE OFFICERS AND ENLISTED MEN
OF THE THIRTEENTH REGIMENT U.S. INFANTRY
IN THE CAMPAIGN AGAINST SANTIAGO DE CUBA
FIRST AT SAN JUAN HILL  JULY 1ST 1898
AS THEY WERE AT VICKSBURG IN 1863

# Buffalo's disappearing twenty-ton rock

In front of the Buffalo History Museum rests the Houdini of rocks. Native Americans believe it's impregnated with spirits and possesses magic properties. It mysteriously vanished sometime between 1955 and 1957, and the Historical Society even placed a chain link security fence around it for more than 50 years.

Purchased in part with money raised by a school children's penny drive in 1898, a monument was to be presented as a tribute to the Thirteenth United States Regiment based at Fort Porter. Over the objections of local Native Americans, a twenty-ton granite boulder was moved from the lower Niagara Gorge near Lewiston to Fort Porter (now Front Park), where a commemorative bronze plaque was attached. Just hours before the monument was to be unveiled for the soldiers, the Regiment received orders which sent it to the Philippines.

Fort Porter was demolished to make way for the International Peace Bridge in 1925. In 1955, when a new approach for the Peace Bridge was built, the bronze plaque was removed, and the boulder was unceremoniously bulldozed under several feet of dirt.

In 1957, the monument was discovered missing, dug up and moved to its current location in front of the History Museum. A new plaque was made bearing the original wording, with one additional line: "Rededicated by the Buffalo Historical Society 1958."

7

**Memorial to the Thirteenth United States Regiment**
The Buffalo History Museum
One Museum Court, Buffalo, NY 14216

# Get a raise

Simple instructions are written at the corner of Main and Huron. Follow them and you will get a raise. Unfortunately it's only about 20 inches.

Skillfully shoe-horned into an awkward lot created by the geometry of Joseph Ellicott's radial street plan sits Buffalo's oldest savings bank and one of its best known landmarks. Opened in 1901, "the bank with the gold dome" was designed by Green and Wicks and constructed for the Buffalo Savings Bank. The sandstone landing at its main entrance proudly announces in large brass letters: "Steps to Success."

The bank's elaborate interior features ceilings and walls that are a pictorial history of Buffalo. The paintings by William Francis, Eugene Savage and George Davidson were not finished until 1926.

Chartered in 1846, Buffalo Savings Bank was the first savings bank in the city. It began with just six depositors, one of whom was the sole employee of the bank. Among the founding trustees was Millard Fillmore, who became the 13th president of the United States. In the 1980s rapid growth and broader national exposure brought the bank a new corporate name: Goldome. In 1990 it was sold to M&T Bank, and became known as M&T Center.

The bank's signature dome was constructed using 13,500 interlocking terra-cotta tiles, engineered to overlap. The tiles were originally overlaid with copper. Much like the copper-clad Statue of Liberty which is also ravaged by oxidation, the dome eventually took on a greenish hue. It has since been gilded with pure gold three time's in 1954, 1979, and 1998. According to the bank, the last restoration required 140,000 toilet paper-thin sheets of 23.75 carat gold leaf at a cost of a half million dollars.

**8**

**"Steps to Success"**
M&T Center
One Fountain Plaza, Buffalo, NY 14202

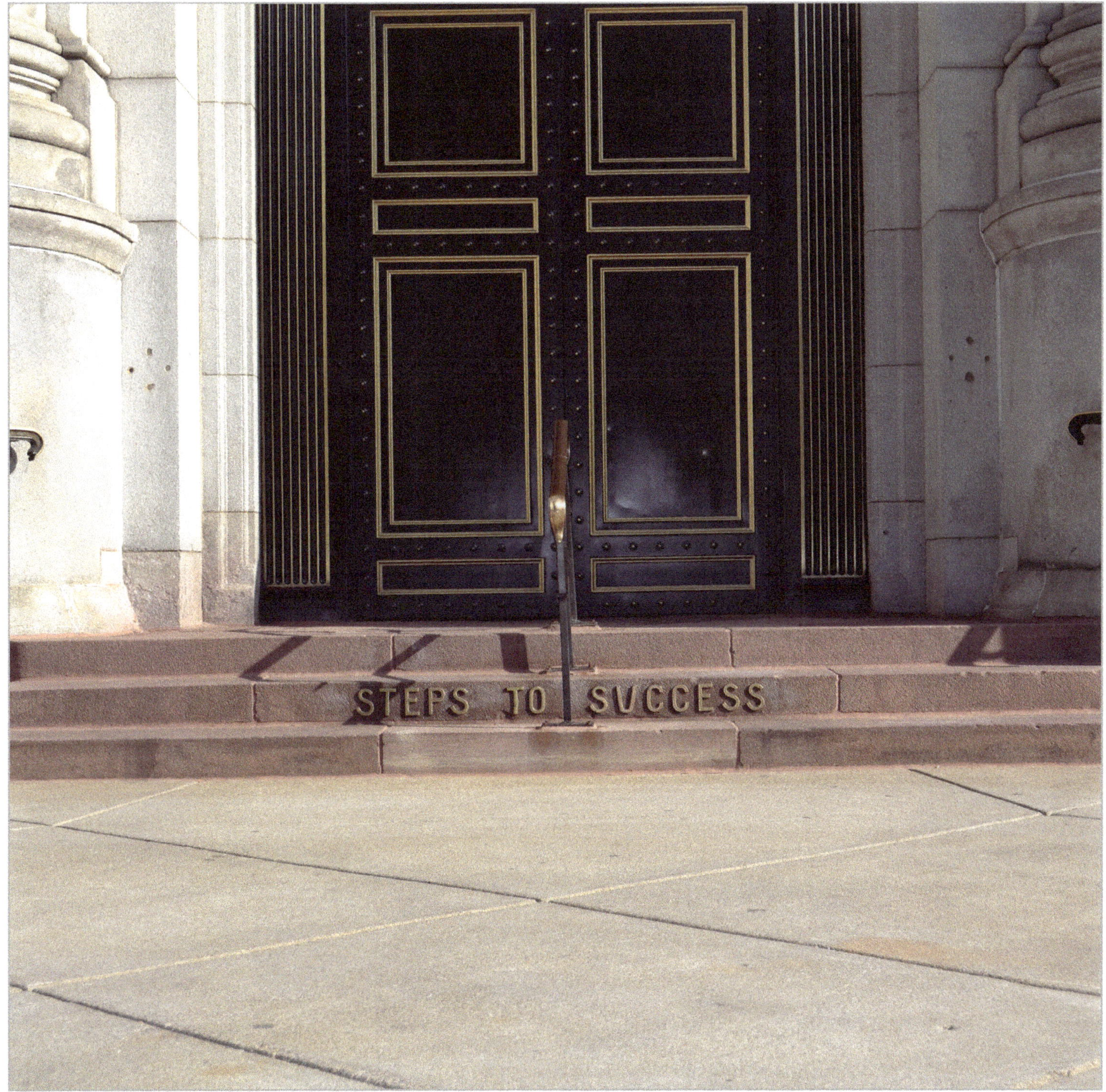

STEPS TO SVCCESS

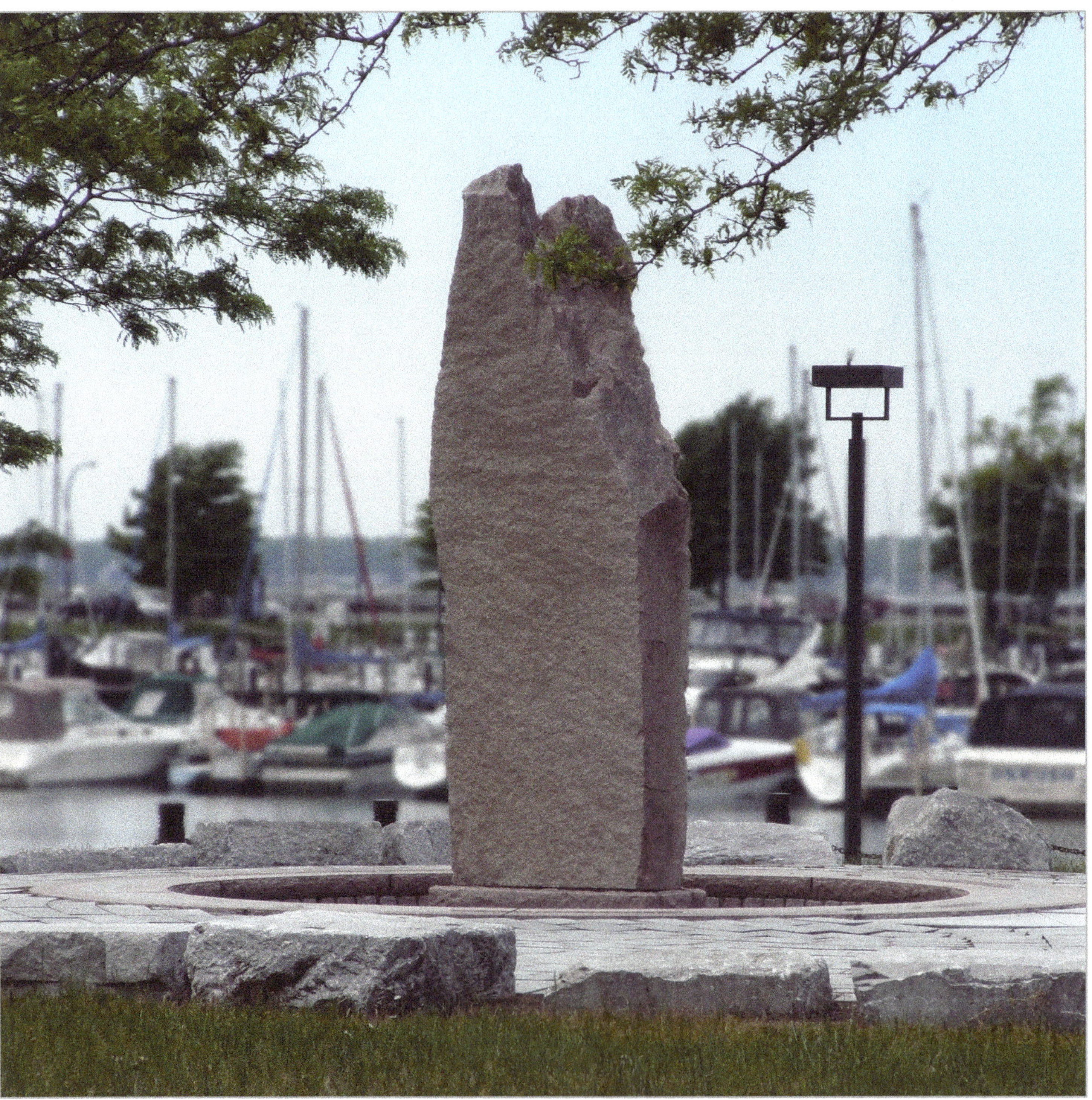

# Irish eyes

It's a secret known by our vast population of gulls, but can be seen by anyone flying overhead. Erie Basin Marina was built in the shape of a Buffalo, and the Buffalo's eye is created by the circular Irish Famine Memorial.

Ireland suffered a Great Famine beginning in 1845 when the potato crop failed. This resulted in the deaths of more than one million people and forced the emigration of nearly two million more.

The Buffalo Waterfront from the mid-to late-19th century became a major inland immigration port. Immigrants from Ireland sailed across the Atlantic to the eastern ports of North America and many continued onward to Western New York. Thousands of Irish settled here near the site of this monument.

The Western New York Irish Famine Memorial is literally in the shadow of the grain and steel mills, the Erie Canal, and other industry magnets that flourished with the influx of cheap, hard-working Irish labor. It is here that the Irish lived, worked and built solid futures for their families.

Perhaps a quote at the memorial says it best."Through hard work and perseverance, the Irish enriched the cultural tapestry of the people of Western New York and left a lasting legacy."

**9**

**Irish Famine Memorial, by Rob Ferguson**
Erie Basin Marina, Buffalo, NY 14202

# Hogwarts

While standing in the shadow of the soaring twin gothic towers that rise above the city's Elmwood Village, close your eyes for just a moment. With a little imagination you can almost picture Harry Potter riding his Nimbus 2000 broomstick between them in hot pursuit of the Golden Snitch.

If you open your eyes and can still see him, please bear in mind that this is the former Buffalo State Asylum for the Insane.

Now referred to as the Richardson Olmsted Complex, this massive group of structures is highlighted by its iconic towers and five wards progressively set back on each side – eleven connected buildings in total. Patients were segregated by sex, males on the east side, females on the west. Tragically, the complex deteriorated severely after patients were moved out during the mid-1970s and the complex remained vacant.

Designed by Henry Hobson Richardson, with grounds by landscape architect Frederick Law Olmsted and Calvert Vaux, the Richardson Olmsted Complex was listed on the National Register of Historic Places in 1986. Built between 1870 and 1896, it was Richardson's first major commission and the first example of a style that has come to be known as Richardson Romanesque.

After many years of fits and starts, a long-stalled renovation has begun with the allocation of $76 million in state funding. Rehabilitating the Richardson Olmsted Complex and reviving its original Olmsted and Vaux landscape will do more than just save an historic landmark. Along with Frank Lloyd Wright's Darwin Martin House and Louis Sullivan's Guaranty Building, the Richardson Olmsted Complex completes the trifecta of Buffalo's most prized architectural treasures.

**10**

**The Richardson Olmsted Complex**
400 Forest Avenue, Buffalo, NY 14213

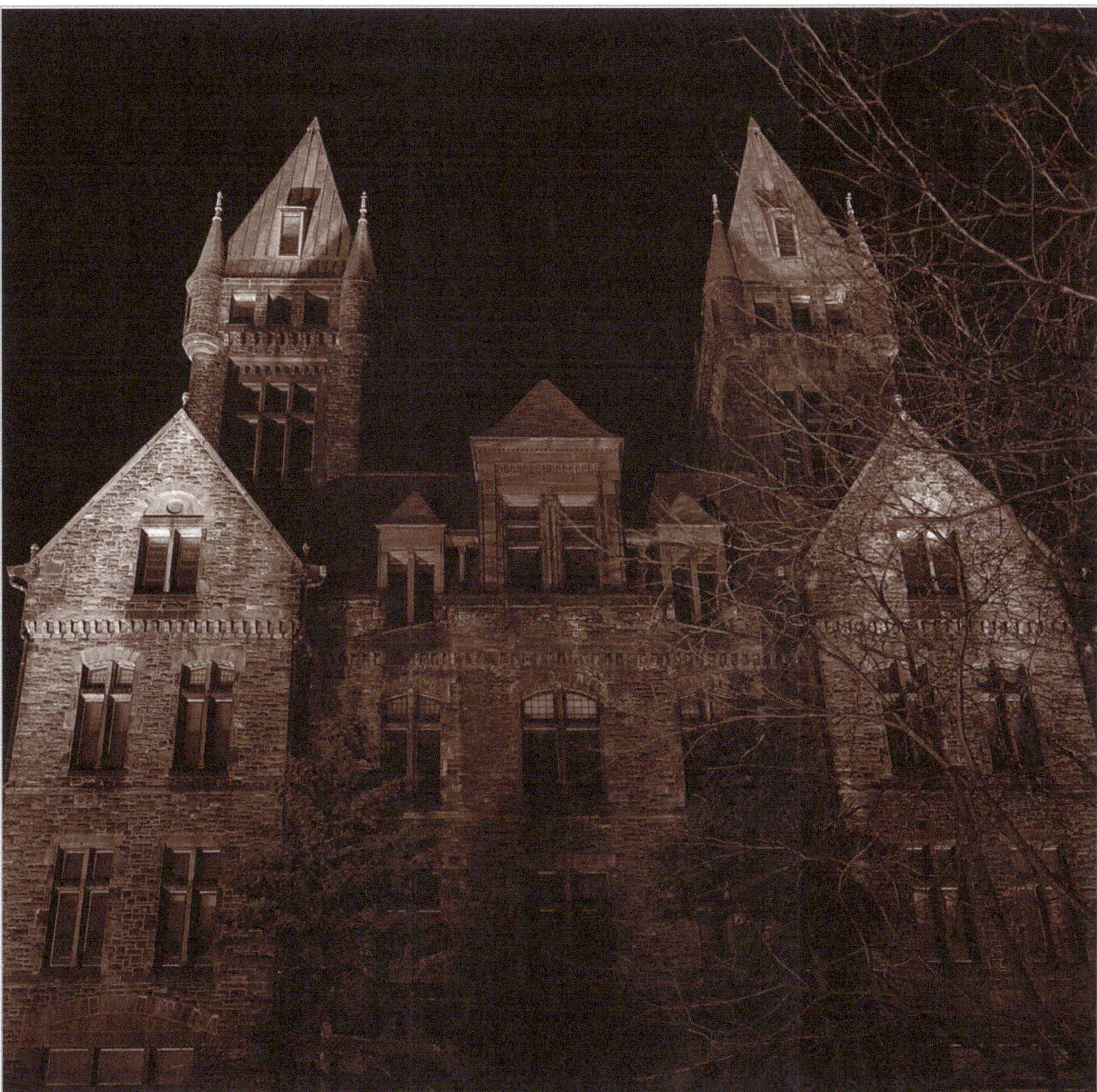

# Furniture built to last beyond a lifetime

A private mausoleum at Forest Lawn Cemetery built in 1988 features a less-than-comfortable polished black granite couch and an S-shaped tête-à-tête sofa. It answers an age-old question; how do you decorate a 269-acre living room? It lacks only a marble remote control and large flat screen TV for the late Chester and Gloria Stachura to be prepared to host all 152,000 of their no longer the life of the party neighbors.

While at first blush stone furniture at a cemetery may seem a bit unusual, it actually embraces the true spirit of its surroundings. In a tradition that began more than 150 years ago, Forest Lawn remains a vital place where past and present are joined and visitors are warmly welcomed. Picnics, tours, and creative events held there enrich the life of the community. Such activities foster the ultimate tribute: those departed are surrounded by vibrant life, ensuring that they are perpetually remembered.

Forest Lawn's great tradition of welcoming visitors grew out of a concept that originated at Père-Lachaise in 1805. This Parisian cemetery was the first to create a park-like space with bucolic vistas intended to attract the living. It encouraged families to visit and remember their loved ones. Forest Lawn became one of the first such cemetaries in America, inviting the public to enjoy its beauty and celebrate its residents.

**11**

**Forest Lawn Cemetery**
114 Delaware Avenue, Buffalo, NY 14202

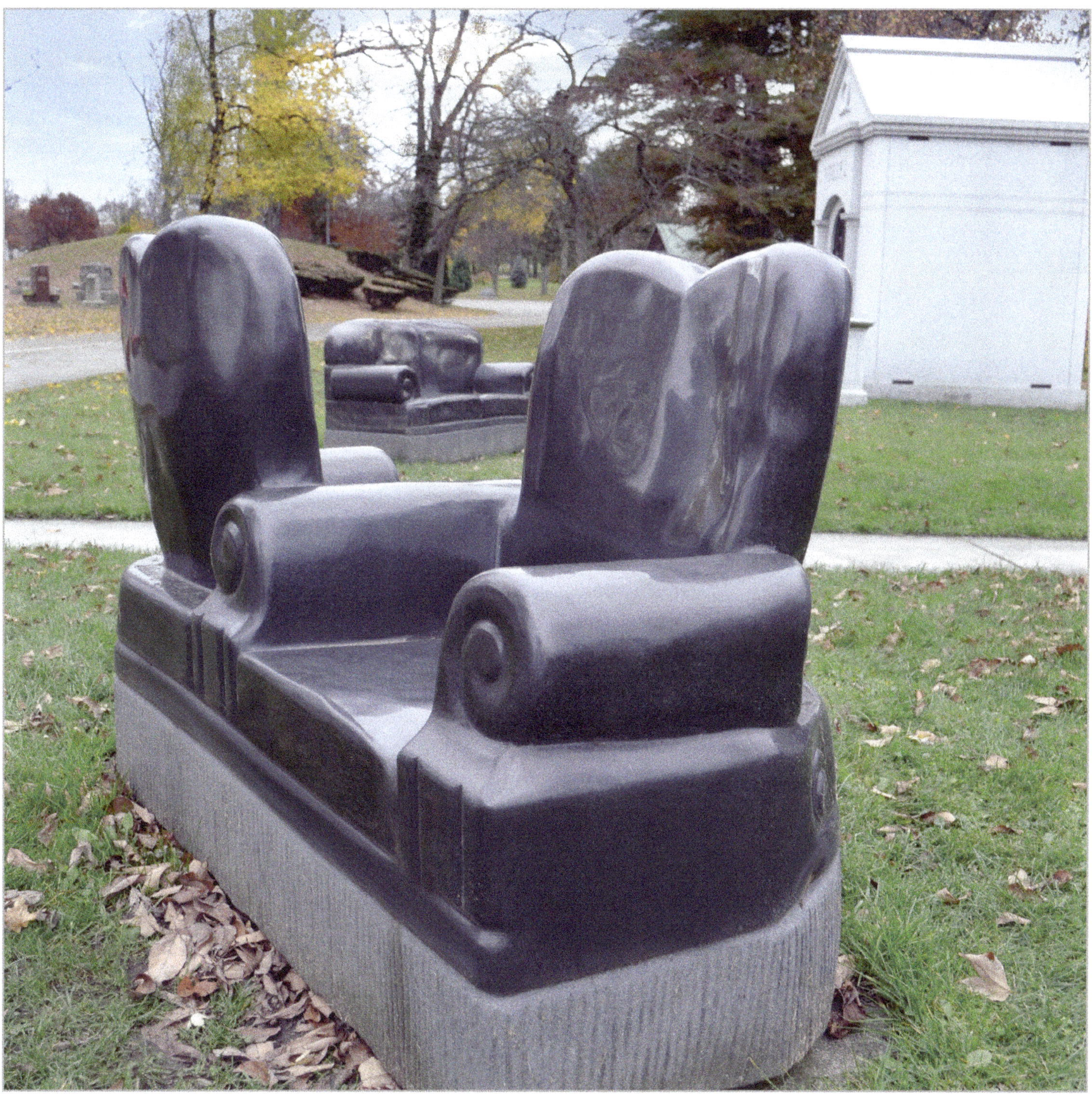

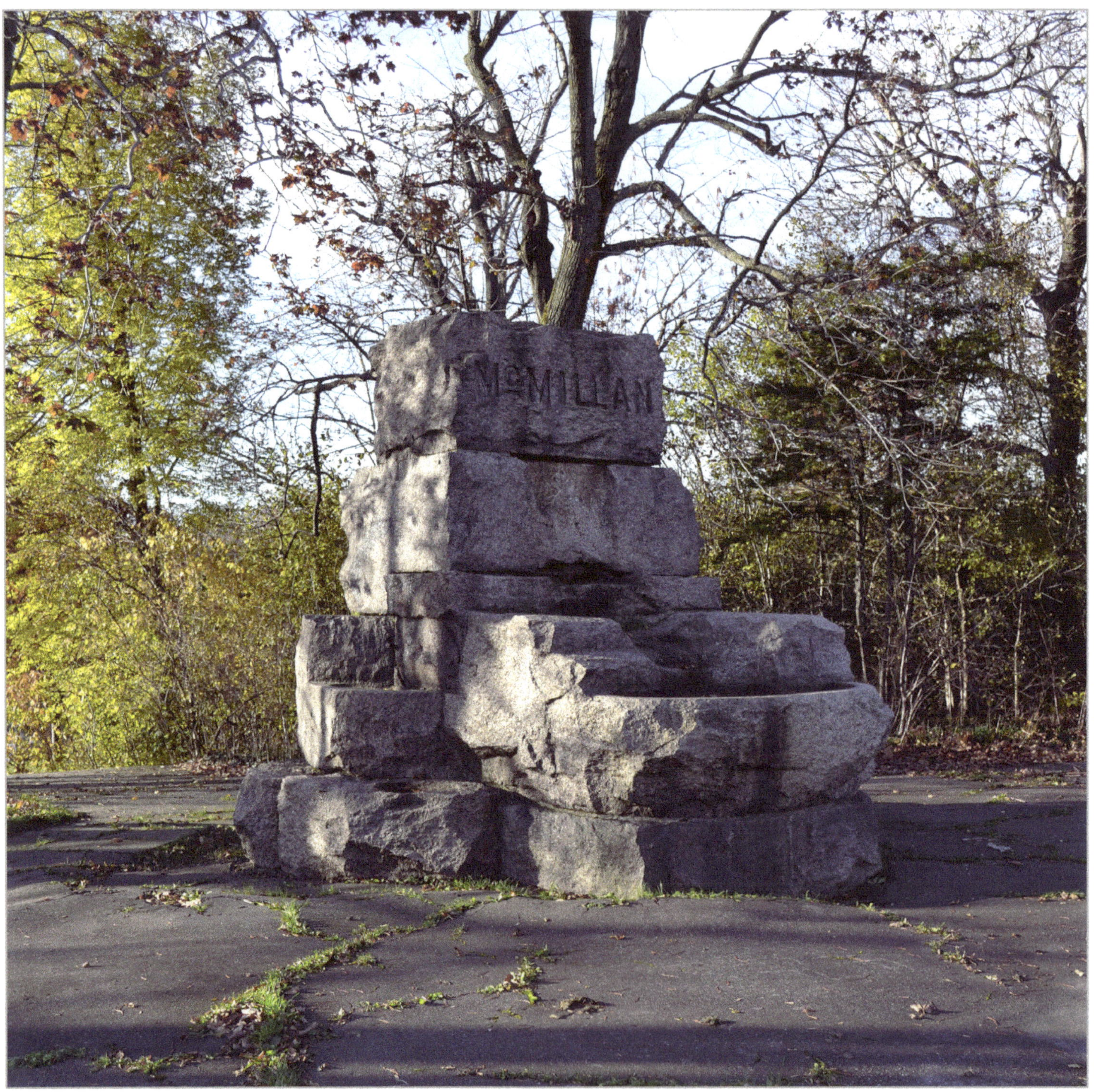
McMILLAN

# The filling station next to the off-ramp

As you exit the westbound Scajaquada Expressway on to Delaware Avenue, blink and you've missed it. Look for it and you still might miss it, or just confuse it for a pile of rocks. This is actually a fountain dedicated to the late William McMillan, the first Superintendent of Buffalo Parks (1870-1898). Built from blocks of granite, it was a place where park visitors, horses, dogs, and birds could stop for a sip of water.

On the back of the fountain is a curious inscription that ends with the words, "Erected by a Few of His Friends -1905."  This is indicative of the love/hate conflict that perenially surrounded the socially awkward McMillan. You either admired his passion for his craft, or his snarky dogma quickly got under your skin.

Fredrick Law Olmsted personally recommended William McMillan for the job that he poured his heart and soul into for 27 years. He was the consummate perfectionist, flawlessly maintaining the parks he cherished. While his skills were many, McMillan steadfastly refused to play along with the politics that increasingly surrounded the parks. He was described as stubborn, obstinate, and "ugly honest," qualities that can literally become a fatal flaw. He was fired from his position in 1897 by the Parks Commission and died just a few months later.

In the words of Parks Commissioner Andrew Langdon, who ironically voted to sack McMillan, "Let us remember that no memorial is more beautiful, no tribute more lasting, than the lovely surroundings of nature, radiant with life and beauty encircling this spot, which was first improved by the hand and brain of Buffalo's first superintendent of parks." Landon helped raise the funds to erect the tribute to McMillan.

**12**

**McMillan Fountain**
Delaware Park
Scajaquada Expressway near the Delaware Avenue exit, Buffalo, NY 14214

# UB wasn't built in a day

The picturesque columns at Baird Point on the University at Buffalo's North Campus are a classic making-lemonade-out-of-lemons story. Baird Point is on Lake LaSalle, a 60-acre, man-made lake built to provide flood control and water runoff, and the iconic columns are from the facade of a bank slated for demolition in 1959.

You can tell how old someone is by where they first remember seeing these columns.

If you were born after 1978, your memories are confined to the current Greek-style amphitheater at Baird Point. It's a great spot for taking a break from studies – from the solitude of watching ducks, geese, and herons, to the infinitely less quiet Student Association's annual Springfest and Fallfest celebrations.

If you're a little older, born between 1959 and 1977, you probably remember these columns covered with paint and graffiti, unceremoniously stacked on South Campus between Schoellkopf Hall and Baird Music Hall. It was a popular student hangout for drinking beer, reading, and drinking more beer.

And if you are really old (born between 1914-1959) you remember these 35-foot columns on the front of The Manufacturers and Traders Bank (M&T Bank) on the corner of Main and Swan Streets in downtown Buffalo, which later became the Federal Reserve Bank.

**13**

**Baird Point**
University at Buffalo - North Campus
Amherst, NY 14260

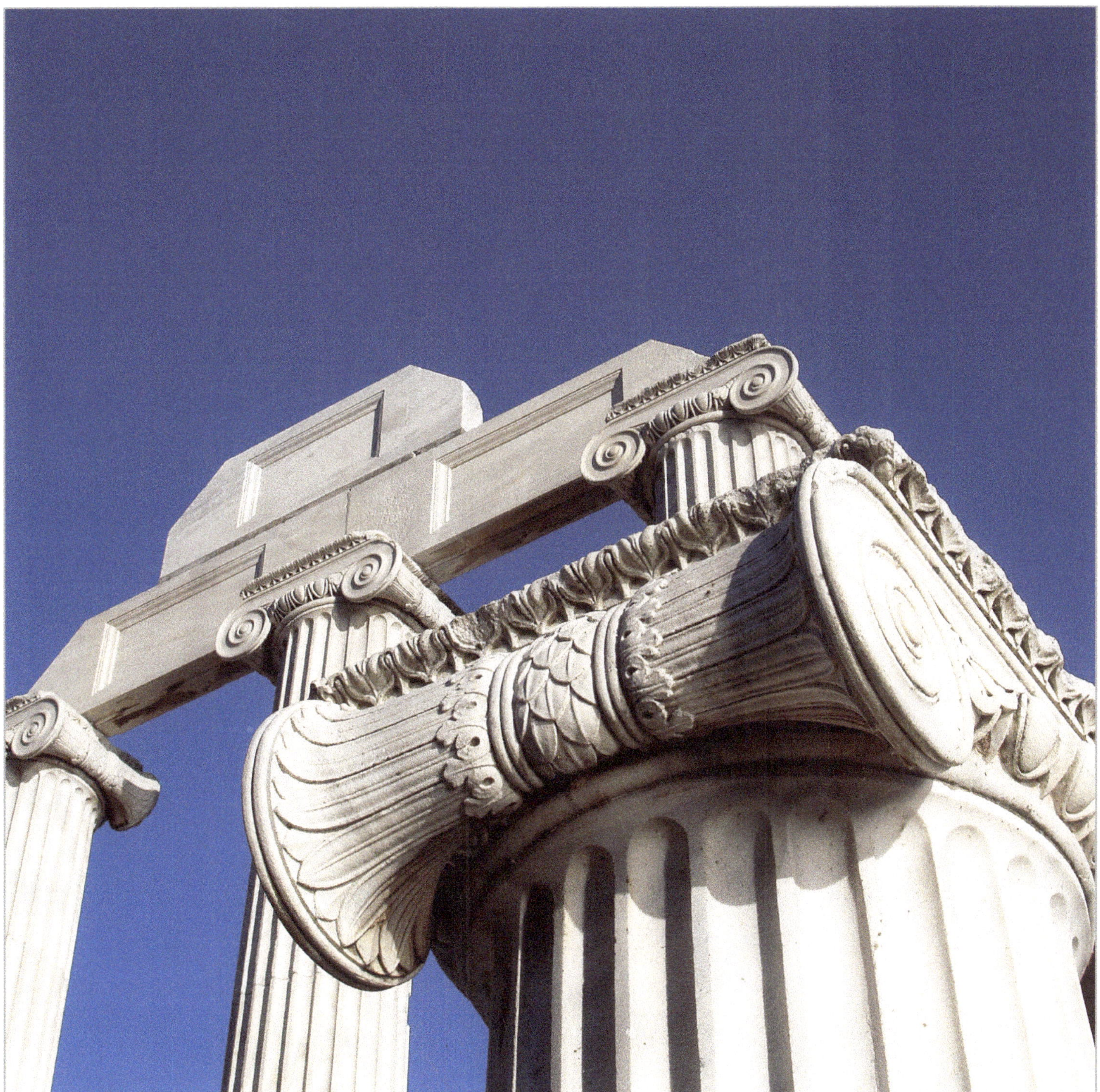

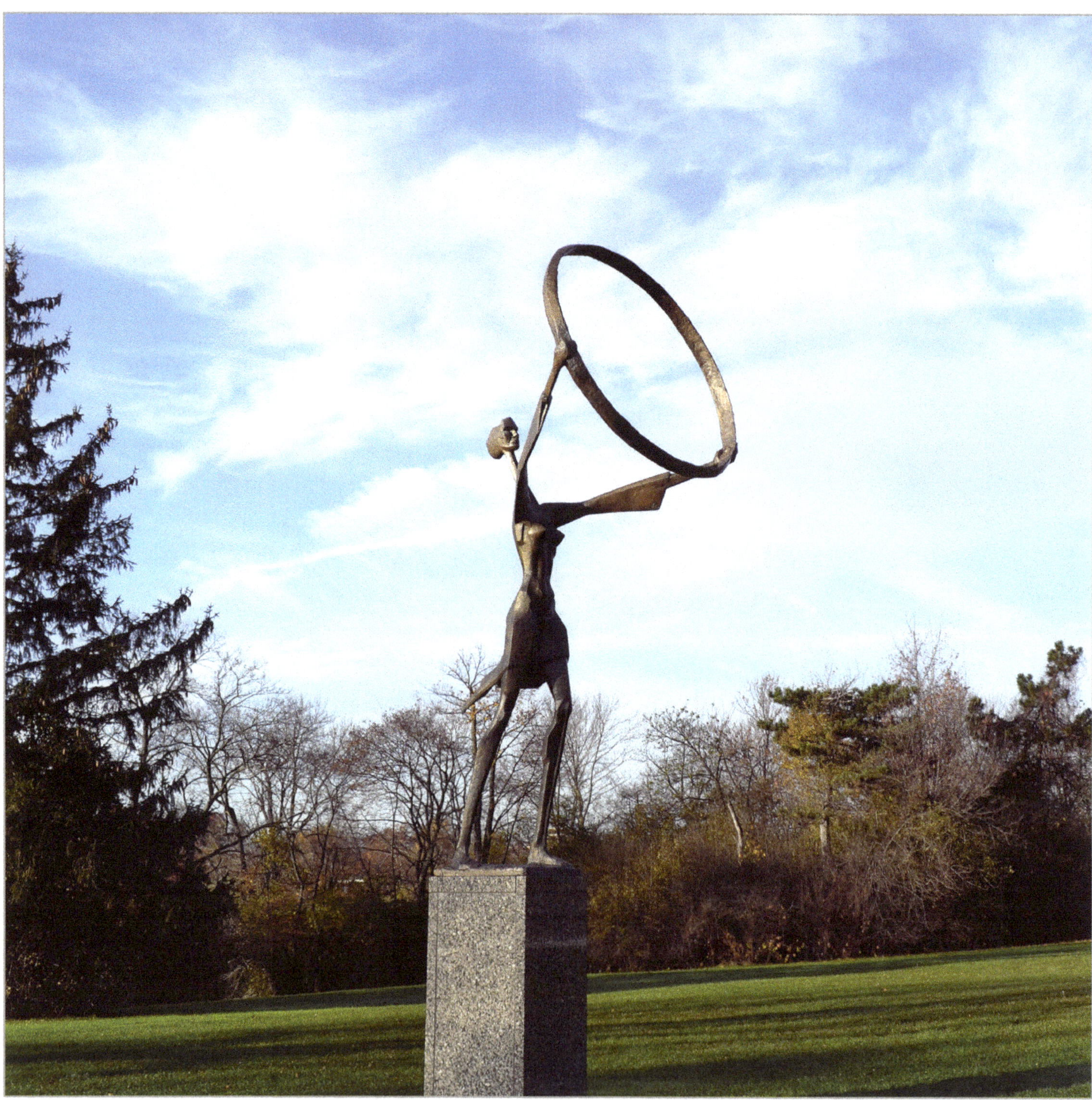

# Anorexic with a hula-hoop

When sculptor and art teacher Larry W. Griffis Jr. (1924-2000) won the commission for a statue depicting "The Spirit of Womanhood," his design was not met with profound silence. Griffis had designed an extremely elongated abstraction of a female figure with arms outstretched above her head to memorialize playwright and Zonta Club founder Marian De Forest. The statue holds a six-foot-diameter hoop meant to represent the world and the circle of existence.

"Exciting," said the Parks Commissioner. "Great possibilities," said the director of the Albright-Knox Art Gallery.

On the other side of the dust-up was a chorus of detractors lobbing jibes like "hideous," and "she's in the terminal stage of some dreadful and wasting disease."

The cruelest cut of all came from a letter to the editor that barbed, "It reminds me of my first wife's mother."

So what was Griffis reaction to this cultural kerfuffle?

"This is the function of art," Griffis said, "to make people think and get excited, to show new concepts. Controversy has gone on ever since artists began creating things. If we put up a figure everybody understands and likes, people would just look at it and say, 'uh-huh, they've got the statue up. That's nice.' But if you put up a controversial piece, now you've got people thinking."

**"The Spirit of Womanhood," by Larry W. Griffis**
Delaware Park near Scajaquada Expressway, Buffalo, NY 14214

# There's a time and place for everything

Erie County Hall is one of Buffalo's best examples of High Victorian Gothic architecture. Completed in 1876, it originally held offices for the City of Buffalo and Erie County. City offices moved to Buffalo City Hall in 1932.

Erie County Hall's most prominent feature is its seven-story clock and bell tower with four nine-feet diameter clocks, which were originally illuminated by gas jets. At one time the tower also held an observatory.

Gracing the corners of the clock tower are four 16-foot tall granite sculptures representing Justice, Mechanical Arts, Agriculture, and Commerce. In 1974 the four female statues were removed to repair their pedestals. When they were returned to their perches, Commerce and Agriculture were placed in the wrong positions. After this unintentional game of musical chairs, the statue of Commerce now enjoys a commanding view of the waterfront from its new southwest corner.

This building has a storied history. The political careers of Presidents Grover Cleveland and Millard Fillmore both began here as mayors of Buffalo.

Assassinated at the Buffalo Pan-American Exposition in 1901, the body of President William McKinley lay In State here in the center of the main lobby. A brass intaglio embedded in the marble floor permanently memorializes the spot where he was placed.

On a granite base in front of County Hall proudly stands a bronze statue of George Washington in full Masonic attire.

**15**

**Justice, Mechanical Arts, Agriculture, and Commerce, by Giovanni F. Sala**
Erie County Hall
92 Franklin Street, Buffalo, NY 14202

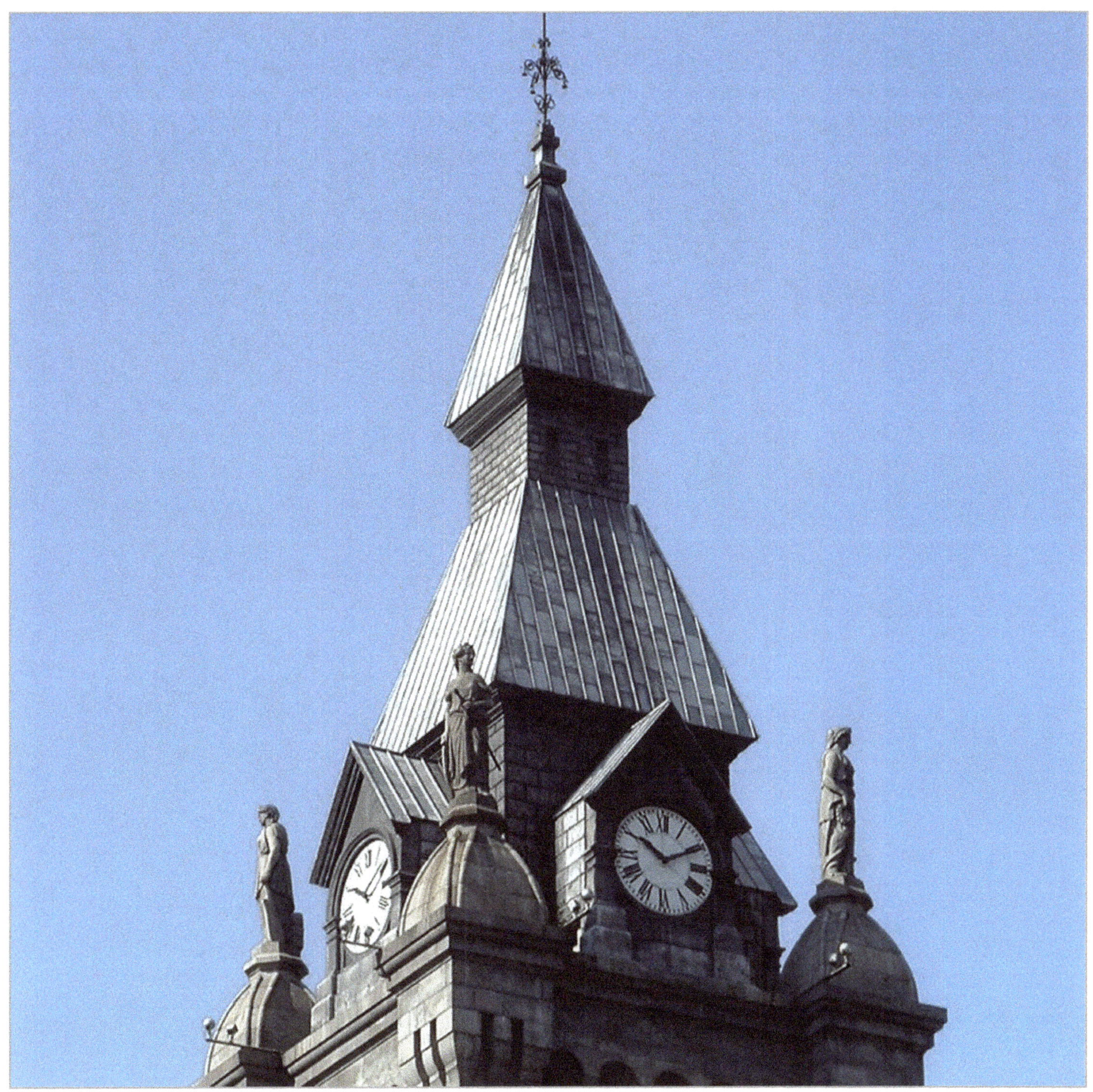

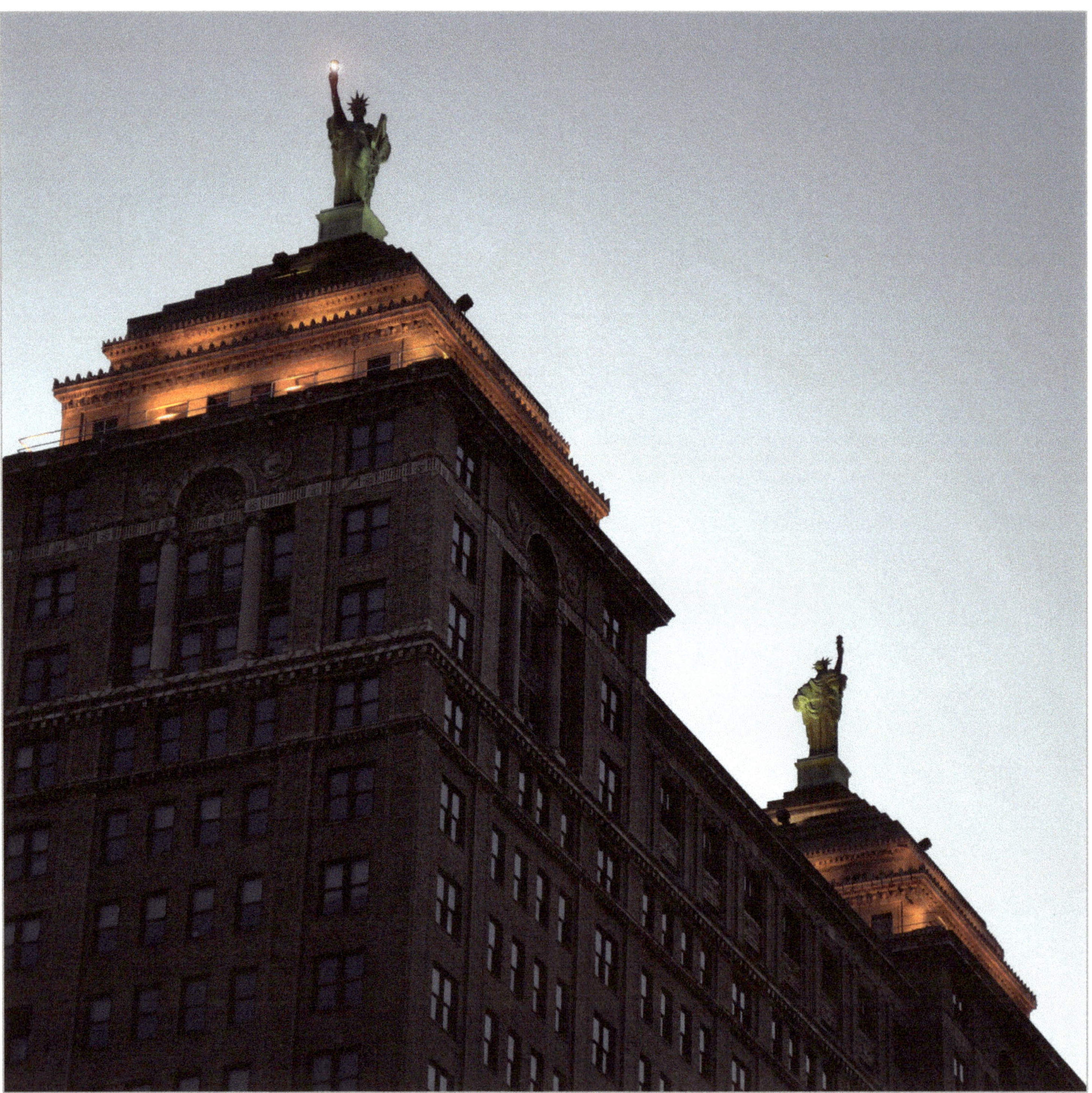

# Buffalo has twice as much liberty as New York City

At one time Buffalo was arguably the center of the known universe. Its prime intermodal location at the terminus of the Erie Canal made it the connecting point between manufacturing in the east and grain coming from the west.

The 23-story Liberty Bank building is crowned with two thirty-six feet replicas of Bartholdi's Statue of Liberty that are illuminated at night. With one facing east and the other facing west, they represent Buffalo's strategic location on the Great Lakes.

At least that's the happy and simple explanation. The real reason represents a darker chapter of our social history.

The building was originally named the German-American Bank. But with the outbreak of World War I came a bigoted reaction to anything German. Sauerkraut was renamed "liberty cabbage," dachshunds became "liberty pups," and the German-American Bank took the name we know it by today: Liberty Bank. While beautifully brightening our skyline, these statues were also unfortunately an overcompensation reflecting the times to appear "more American."

On September 23, 2010 French tightrope walker Didier Pasquette completed a 150-feet walk across a high-wire suspended between the two statues (possibly while eating "Freedom Fries.")

**16**

**Twin Statues of Liberty**
Liberty Bank Building
420 Main Street, Buffalo, NY 14202

# A forefinger of stone

The McKinley Monument is a sleek obelisk in Niagara Square which honors the memory of William McKinley, twenty-fifth President of the United States who was fatally shot while attending the Pan-American Exposition in Buffalo. The monument was dedicated on September 6, 1907, as part of the Buffalo Old Home Week celebration, exactly six years after the tragedy at the Temple of Music on the Exposition grounds. It also coincided with the 75th anniversary of Buffalo's incorporation as a city.

The monument consists of a 96-foot obelisk, surrounded by marble sculptures of sleeping lions, dolphins, and spitting turtles by Alexander Phimister Proctor.

Carl Sandburg wrote a poem about the monument, "Slants at Buffalo, New York."
The poem begins: "A forefinger of stone, dreamed by a sculptor, points to the sky.
It says: This way! This way!"

In 1807 Joseph Ellicott, surveyor and land agent for the Holland Land Co. designed eight streets radiating at equal angles, much like the spokes of a wheel. Niagara Square, with its new location framed by City Hall and two courthouses, defines the center of the city.

Niagara Square has had an interesting evolution. It actually began as a square, but with the advent of cars the square was changed to a circle. And in the summer of 1976 Mayor Stan Makowski began a controversial construction project that involved building a six-feet brick wall around the square's entire circumference. The public overwhelmingly rallied against it, unaffectionately calling it Fort Makowski. Anti-Fort forces even went so far as to drive cardboard-covered cars decorated to look like tanks to demonstrations. That September work ceased, and Niagara Square was returned to its former glory.

On October 8, 2011, Occupy Buffalo transformed Niagara Square into an encampment which lasted four months, bringing their message of economic injustice front and center.

**William McKinley Monument, by Alexander Phimister Proctor**
Niagara Square, Buffalo, NY 14202

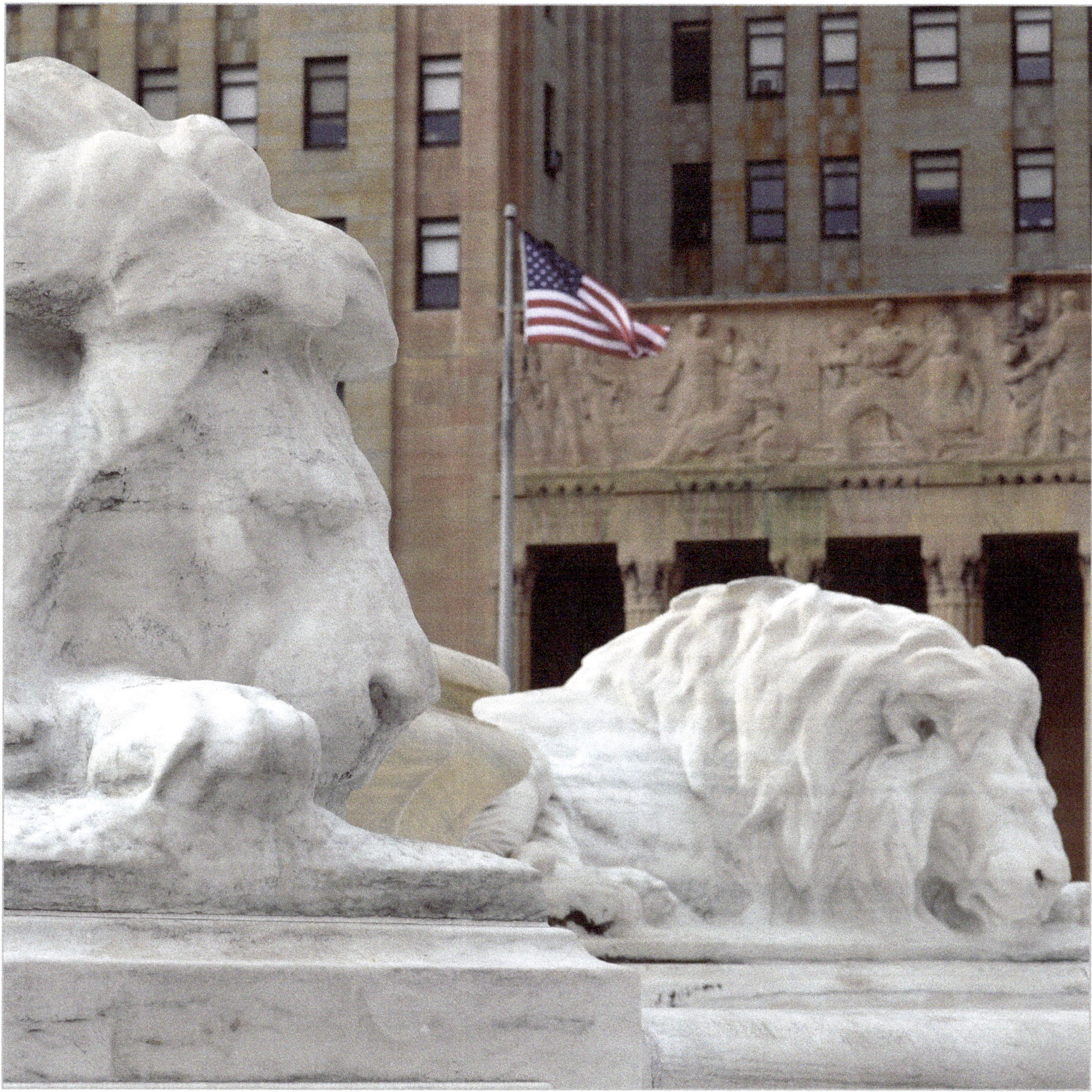

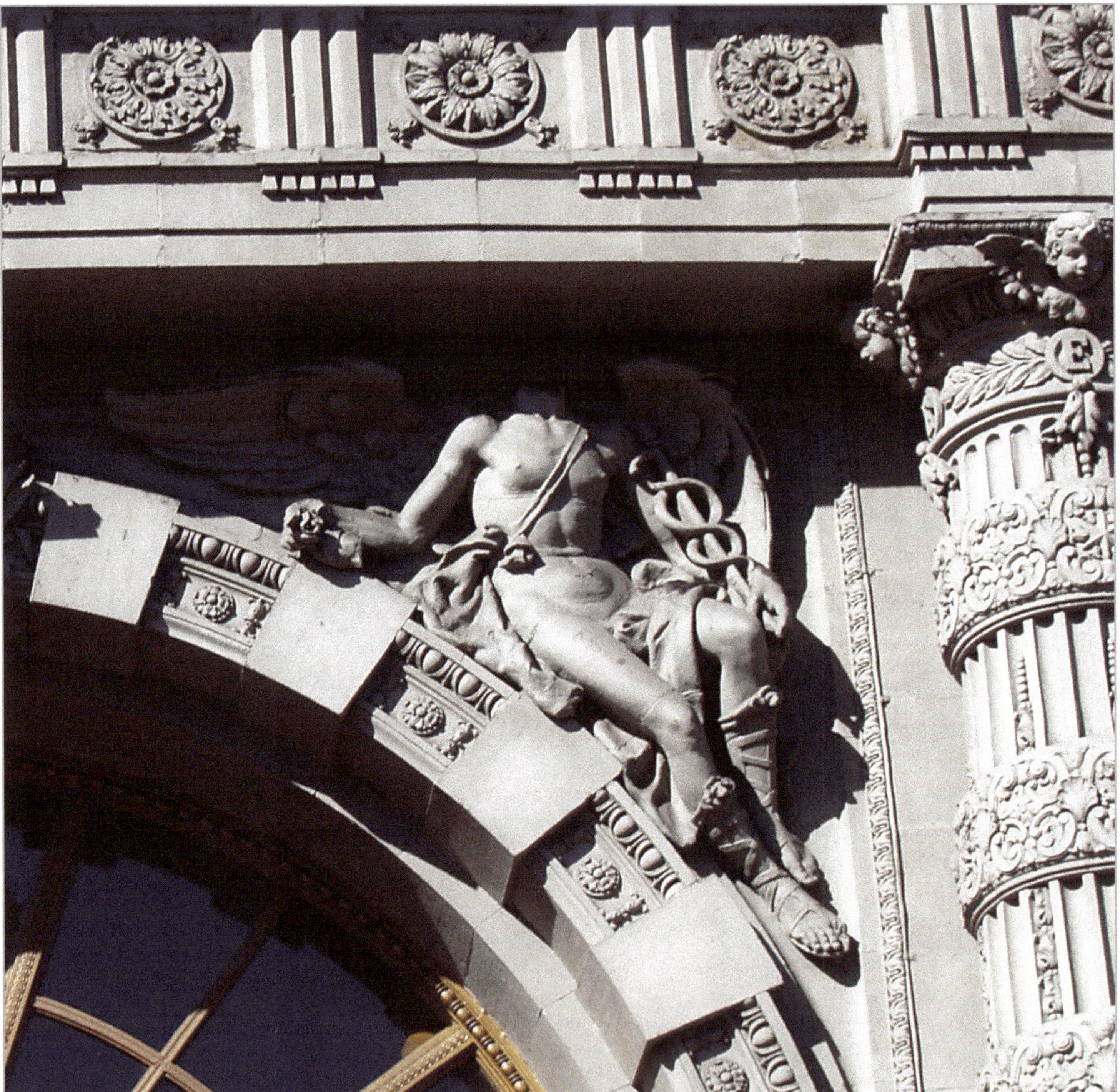

# Where headless angels fear to tread

Architect Daniel Burnham is known for the aphorism: "Make no small plans, they have no magic to stir men's blood; think big." Designed by Charles B. Atwood, Burnham's head of "all artistic matters," the construction of the Ellicott Square Building certainly fulfilled that vision.

Named for Joseph Ellicott, the planner and surveyor who laid out the street plan of Buffalo, the ornate, ten-story, 500,000 square foot building was the largest office building in the world until 1908. Primarily mixed-use office space, in 1984 it was also used for hotel scenes in the movie "The Natural."

Terra-cotta was chosen for Ellicott Square's trademark French Renaissance style ornamentation. Similar to molded clay, terra-cotta can be worked into elaborate figurines and intricate patterns.  Four large caduceus holding figures, an unusual highbred conflation of Mercury and an angel, hover over the doorways to the east and west entrances.

All but one has a head.

The building wasn't always its present day color. It was painted gray in 1971.

18

**Ellicott Square Building - East Entrance**
295 Main Street, Buffalo, NY 14203

# Art on a roll

In 2003, seventy-two Western New York artists set out to reinvent the wheel. When they had finished, it was no longer round.

Art on Wheels was a huge public art project co-sponsored by the Burchfield-Penney Art Center and the Materials Reuse Project roughly based on the 2001 Herd About Buffalo program. It was an exhibition of 125 wheel-themed sculptures and art cars placed in 57 public spaces throughout Erie and Niagara counties. They were displayed at historical, cultural, and heritage host sites that were linked to a mapped arts trail that spanned from Old Fort Niagara in Youngstown to the Graycliff Estate in Derby.

In a city known for its wild imagination, the creativity and diversity of the sculptures and art cars did not disappoint. Artists were able to create their works in 18,000 square feet of free space donated for eight months at the Great Arrow Industrial Park, once home to Buffalo's famed Pierce Arrow car company.

The result was a win-win-win, for the cultural tourists who enjoyed them, for the institutions that benefited from the additional exposure and foot traffic, and for the Burchfield Penney Art Center and the Materials Reuse Project that raised money through the proceeds of the art that was auctioned at the end of the project.

The sculpture on the right is "Red," a fourteen-feet chicken designed by Hamburg artist Debbie Hill. Currently living in Lockport, Red is often pointed out as an attraction during Erie Canal tours. It was constructed from a concrete mixing truck.

**19**

**"Red," by Debbie Hill**
Art On Wheels
Private owners throughout Western New York

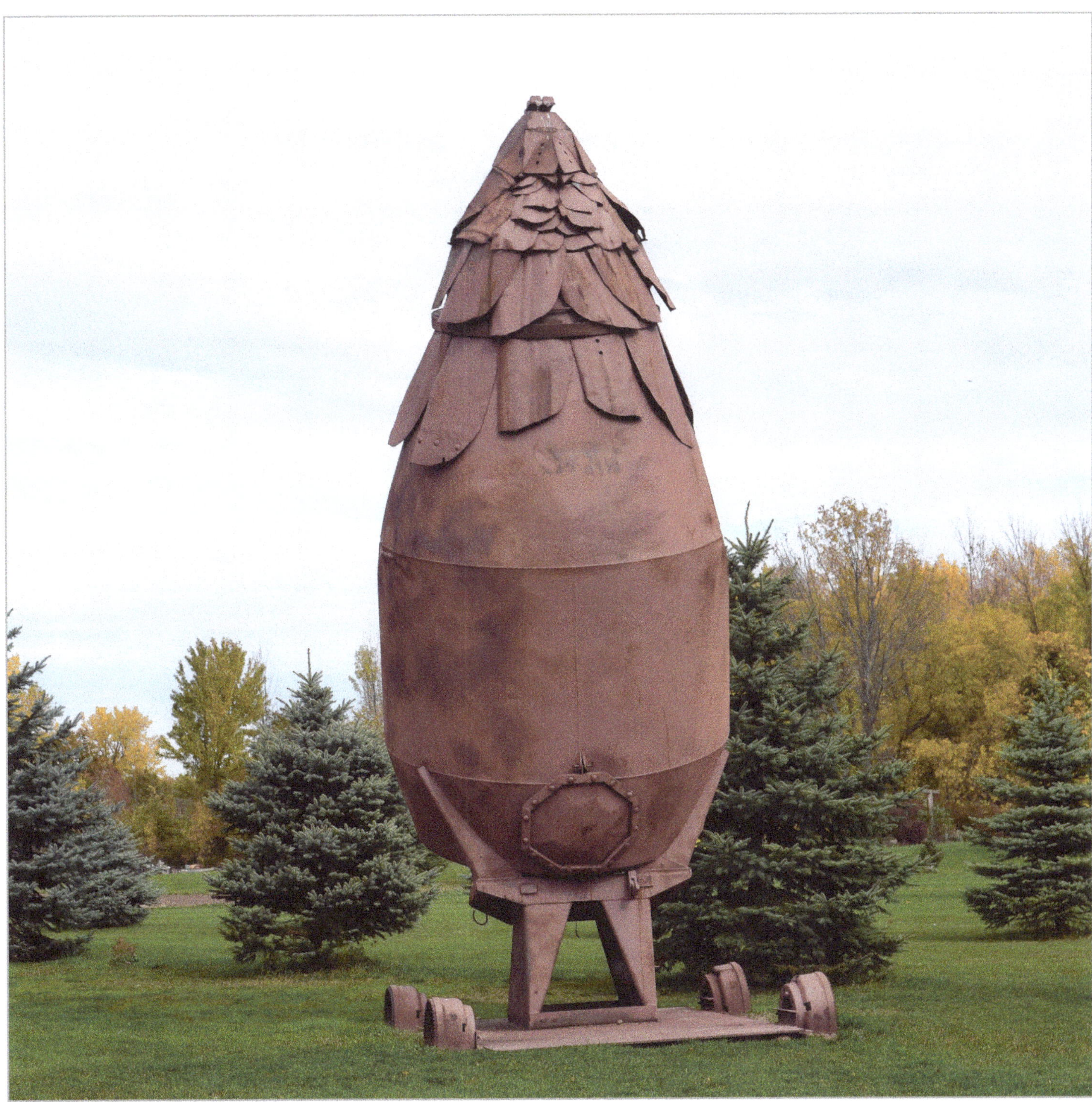

# Frontiers unfettered by any frowning fortress

Buffalo City Hall, a thirty-two-story art deco structure, is the most expensive municipal building ever constructed. It was built in the depths of the Great Depression, back when the dollar was still worth a dollar, at a cost of more than $7 million.

The building was officially dedicated on July 1, 1932, to commemorate the City Centennial. Everywhere you look you see wildly exuberant ornamentation illustrating Buffalo's rich history. Even the symbolism is layered with symbolism.

The exterior is covered with friezes and bas reliefs, and features prominent statues of Millard Fillmore and Grover Cleveland, Buffalonians who became Presidents of the United States.

Inside, on the vaulted ceiling of the lobby, are thousands of terra-cotta tiles intricately designed to resemble an Iroquois chieftan headdress. On the east and west walls are murals by William deLeftwich Dodge, with preposterous alliterative titles like "Frontiers Unfettered by Any Frowning Fortress" and "Talents Diversified Find Vent in Myriad Form."

The ceiling of the Common Council Chamber on the 13th floor is dominated by a jaw-dropping stained glass sunburst skylight. The perimeter of the chamber is circled by what was originally to have been twelve busts of prominent Buffalonians. After heated debate the Council deadlocked on a list of worthy candidates so the busts are now all identical and meant to represent positive virtues.

The perennial joke docents love to tell during this portion of the free tours of the building is that among the noticeably missing virtues are competence, honesty, and thriftiness.

**20**

**"Frontiers Unfettered by Any Frowning Fortress," by William deLeftwich Dodge**
Buffalo City Hall - Main Lobby
65 Niagara Square, Buffalo, NY 14202

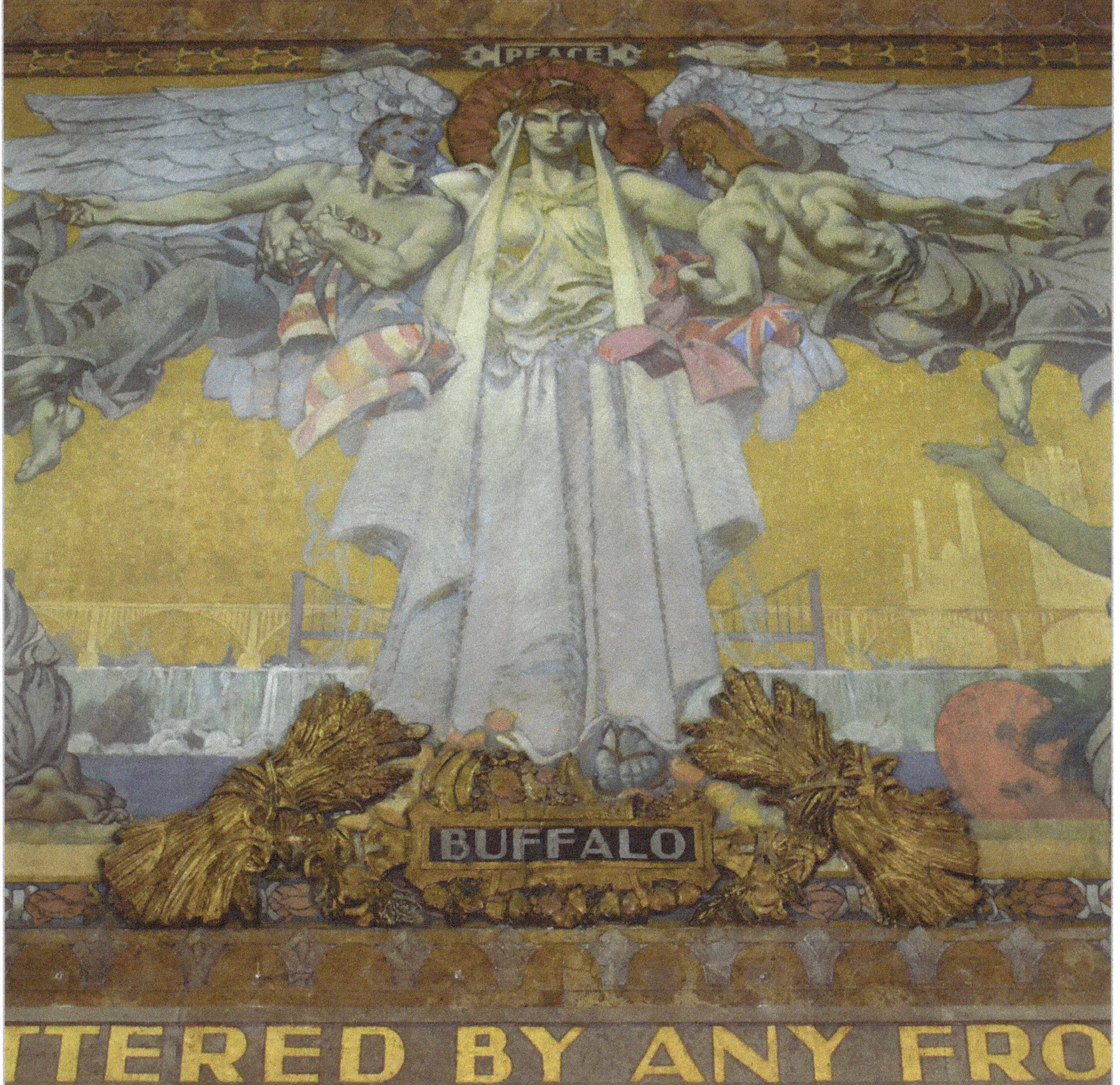
PEACE
BUFFALO
TTERED BY ANY FRO

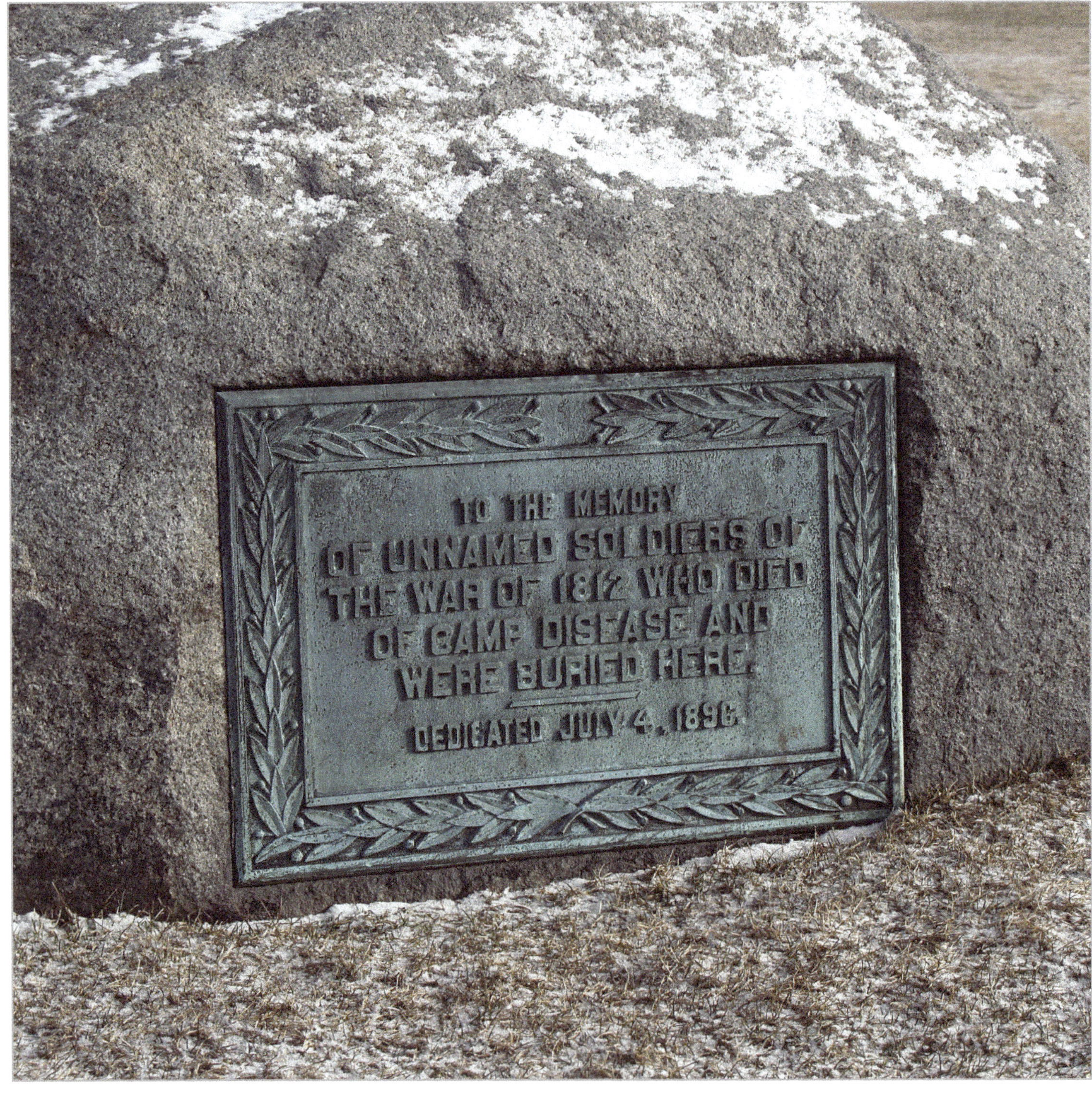

TO THE MEMORY
OF UNNAMED SOLDIERS OF
THE WAR OF 1812 WHO DIED
OF CAMP DISEASE AND
WERE BURIED HERE.
DEDICATED JULY 4, 1896

# An unknown grave for unnamed soldiers

As any hardy Buffalonian will gladly tell you, there is no such thing as cold weather, just inappropriate clothing.

That is a tough lesson that 300 American soldiers who set up camp near the present day Forest Lawn Cemetery in the fall of 1812 would never live to share. They came from Virginia and Maryland wearing summer-weight linen uniforms, many without boots. They lived in open-ended tents and blankets were a scarce luxury. And to top things off, this was an unusually brutal winter, even by Buffalo standards.

Contrary to popular belief, the typical soldier in the War of 1812 did not die from bullets or cannonballs, but rather from dysentery, typhoid ("lake" fever), pneumonia, malaria, measles or smallpox. Of those who died in the war, nearly three-quarters succumbed to something other than a battle wound.

They died at a rate of three or four a day and were initially buried in shallow graves near Scajaquada Creek. In the spring they were reburied in a single mass grave in the center of Delaware Park. Originally the grave site was marked only by two willow trees. After the trees died, and a mere eighty-four years later, a flagpole, a boulder, and a pair of cannon were dedicated to mark the grave. The two cannons and flagpole have long since disappeared leaving only a graffiti-covered boulder near the fourth hole of the Delaware Park Golf Course.

Thanks to the leadership of Steve Cichon, on May 28, 2012, an additional marker at Gate 8 at the Buffalo Zoo directs peoples attention to the boulder marking the War of 1812 Memorial to Unknown Soldiers in the park meadow directly behind them.

**21**

**War of 1812 Memorial to Unknown Soldiers**
Delaware Park - "The Meadows" - Buffalo, NY 14214

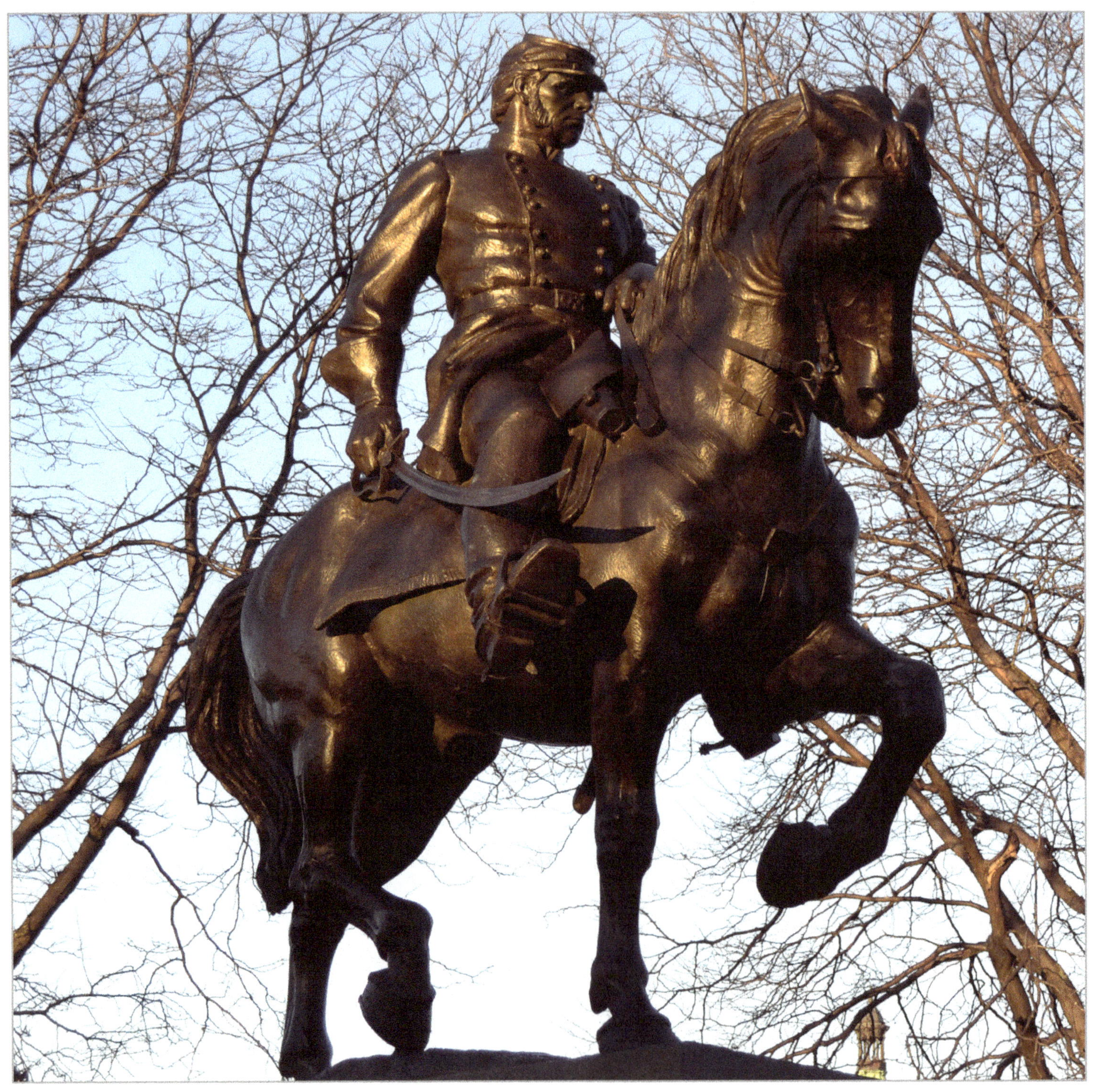

# I give this monument two hoofs up

In the center of Colonial Circle is a one-horse merry-go-round, and the ugly guy with the big bushy sideburns won't let anyone else take a turn. Actually it's an equestrian statue of Brigadier General Daniel Davidson Bidwell who is buried at Forest Lawn Cemetery.

Colonial Circle, once called Bidwell Place, is an Olmsted-designed traffic circle that connects Richmond Avenue with Bidwell Parkway. Almost all map and textbook references to Colonial Circle also contain the words "formerly Bidwell Place." For history wonks, this is curious for several reasons. The street name was unceremoniously changed in 1909 by petition of property owners, meaning there are only a handful of Buffalonian's still alive to be confused. And the choice of the name Colonial is particularly odd considering that during colonial times Buffalo was little more than a tiny French trading post.

Bidwell was mortally wounded in action on October 19, 1864, at the Battle of Cedar Creek in Virginia in the late days of the Civil War. By coincidence his statue has two legs in the air.

There is a popular, but easily debunked urban myth that if the statue's horse is rampant (both front legs in the air), the rider died in battle; one front leg up means the rider was wounded in battle or died of battle wounds; and if the horse is red with all four hooves off the ground you're at a gas station.

As a wimsical sidebar, former Mayor Frank A. Sedita's home was on Colonial Circle. From his front yard he had an interesting view of the part of the horse that goes over the fence last.

**"General Daniel Davidson Bidwell," by Sahl Swarz**
Colonial Circle, Buffalo, NY 14213

# Old-school texting

Ahh, the good old days.

In 1930, texting while driving was absolutely unheard of. Keyboards for text-based messaging had 90 keys, words first had to be cast in molten lead, and it took upwards of twelve hours before the information arrived – delivered by hand.

Newspapers, now called smartphones and iPads, were the social networking tools of the day. They lacked the immediacy that people now take for granted, and would now make the entire Twittersphere go apoplectic.

On the front of the former Courier Express Building there are several terra-cotta relief sculptures which depict the eight basic stages of newspaper development. To produce even a rudementary newspaper in 1930 when the building was constructed required multiple, lengthy steps. This process has been greatly simplified today with the advent of computerized typesetting and offset printing.

The art deco Courier Express building, now headquarters for the Catholic Diocese of Buffalo, was completed in 1930 and was home to the Courier Express Newspaper until the paper ceased publication in 1982. The paper was formed by the merger of two papers: the Buffalo Courier and the Buffalo Express. Mark Twain was once part owner and editor of the Buffalo Express.

**23**

**Bas Relief**
Catholic Diocese Chancery (former Courier Express Building)
785-795 Main Street, Buffalo, NY 14203

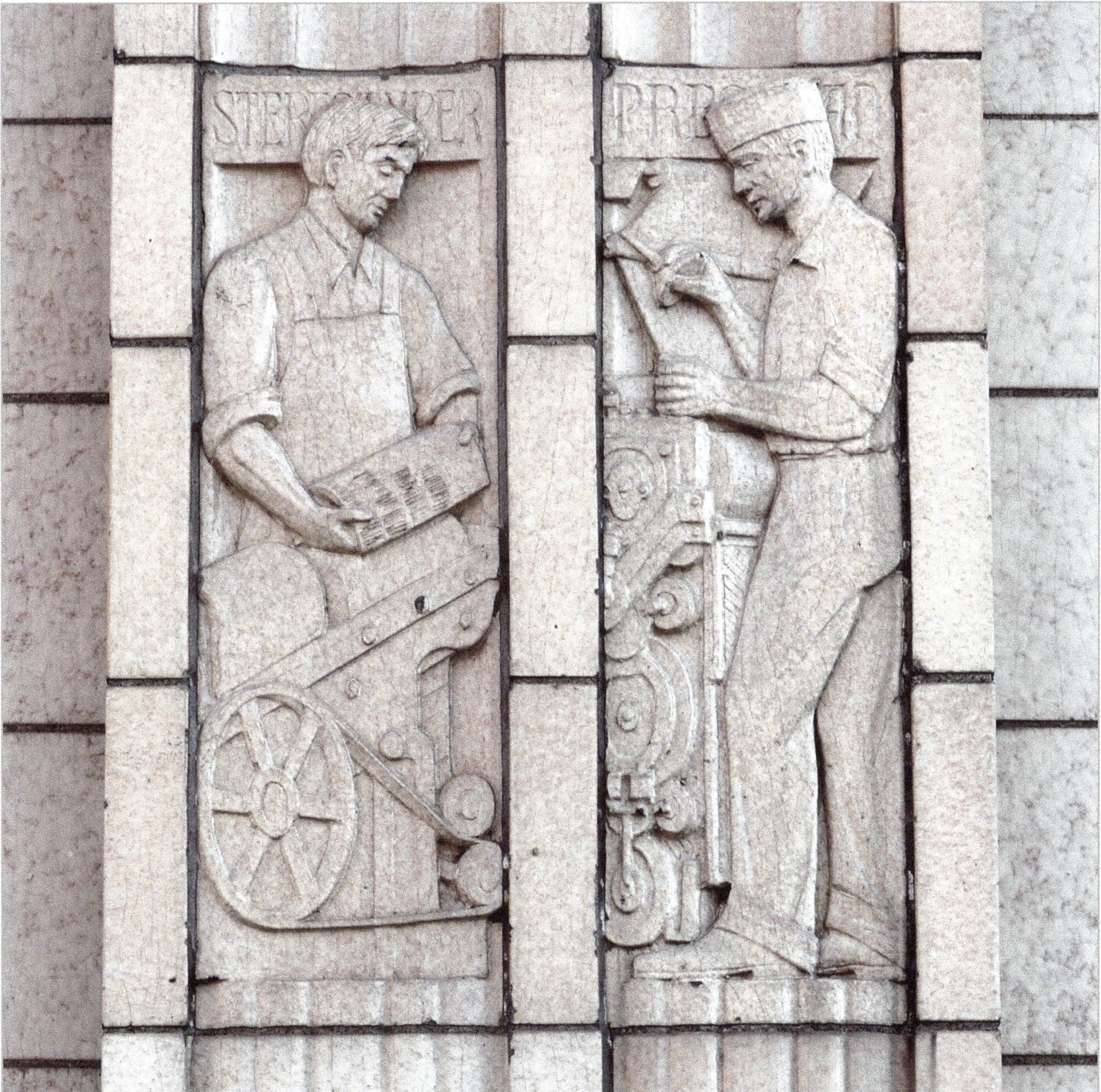
STEREOTYPER
PRESSMAN

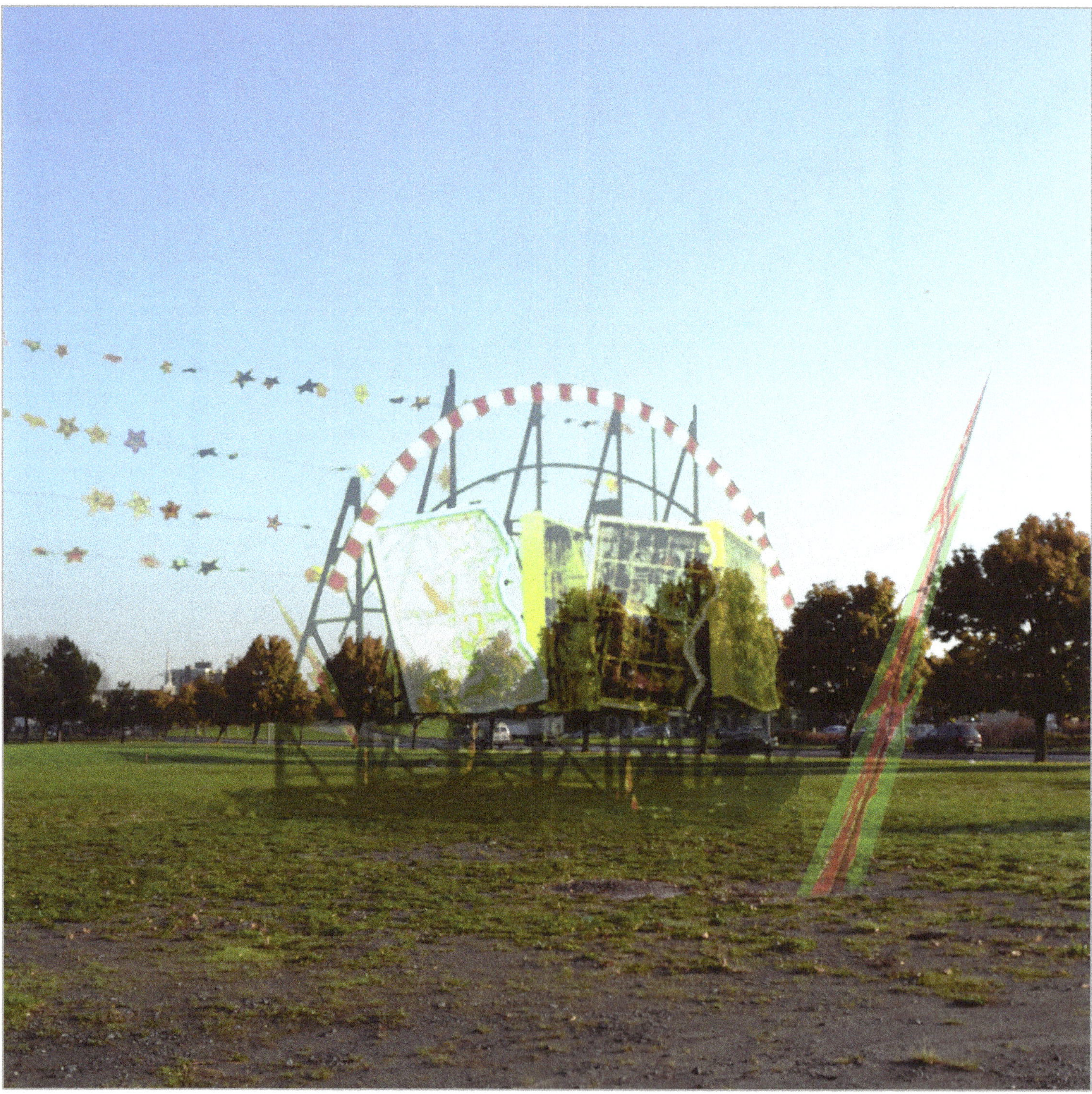

# Astraphobia: the irrational fear of lightning

There was a time in Buffalo when we didn't need soap operas. We had public art.

After two years of preparation, artist Billie Lawless began installing his 180-by-160-feet sculpture in October of 1984 on an empty Urban Renewal Agency-owned lot on Genesee Street between the Elm-Oak Arterial. Named "Green Lightning," it was a parody of a carnival midway. The billboard-style steel framework supported four boxes illuminated with neon, a circus-like arch, and clotheslines hung with decorated, twirling stars. Scattered around the main structure were thirteen day-glow green lightning bolts, some as tall as thirty feet.

It was November 15th when the work was ready. A full slate of dignitaries and the media had assembled on that cold Thursday night for the unveiling. Each took a turn praising the work. Then came the moment of reckoning as the artist flipped the switch. Instantly the lights glowed and jaws collectively dropped.

Turning on the power exposed what most would describe as cartoonish renditions of neon male genitalia sporting top hats and canes. In a 60-second programed sequence, the glowing tallywackers did a brief dance and hat-doffing bow in true Fred Astaire style. According to Lawless, these "abstracted dancing figures celebrating life" were adapted from graffiti drawings he found on the side of an abandoned building on Bailey Avenue. The plug was pulled after a mere 15 minutes.

At the speed of light, a finger-pointing-feeding-frenzy broke out. The Buffalo Arts Commission swore it was a "hoax" and that they had been duped. Lawless claimed that the sculpture was precisely the same as the scaled models and renderings he had presented on multiple occasions.

Hizzoner, Mayor Jimmy Griffin, decided to take things into his own hands. He ordered a sign company to dismantle the sculpture under the cloak of darkness. The destruction was stopped when New York State Supreme Court Justice Vincent Doyle issued an injunction and publicly denounced the actions of the Mayor.

"Green Lightning" was eventually relocated to Chicago where it was shown for ten years without a shred of controversy. It is currently in storage in Cleveland, Ohio.

**24**

**"Green Lightning," by Billie Lawless**
Formerly on Genesee St. between the Elm-Oak Arterial, Buffalo, NY 14202

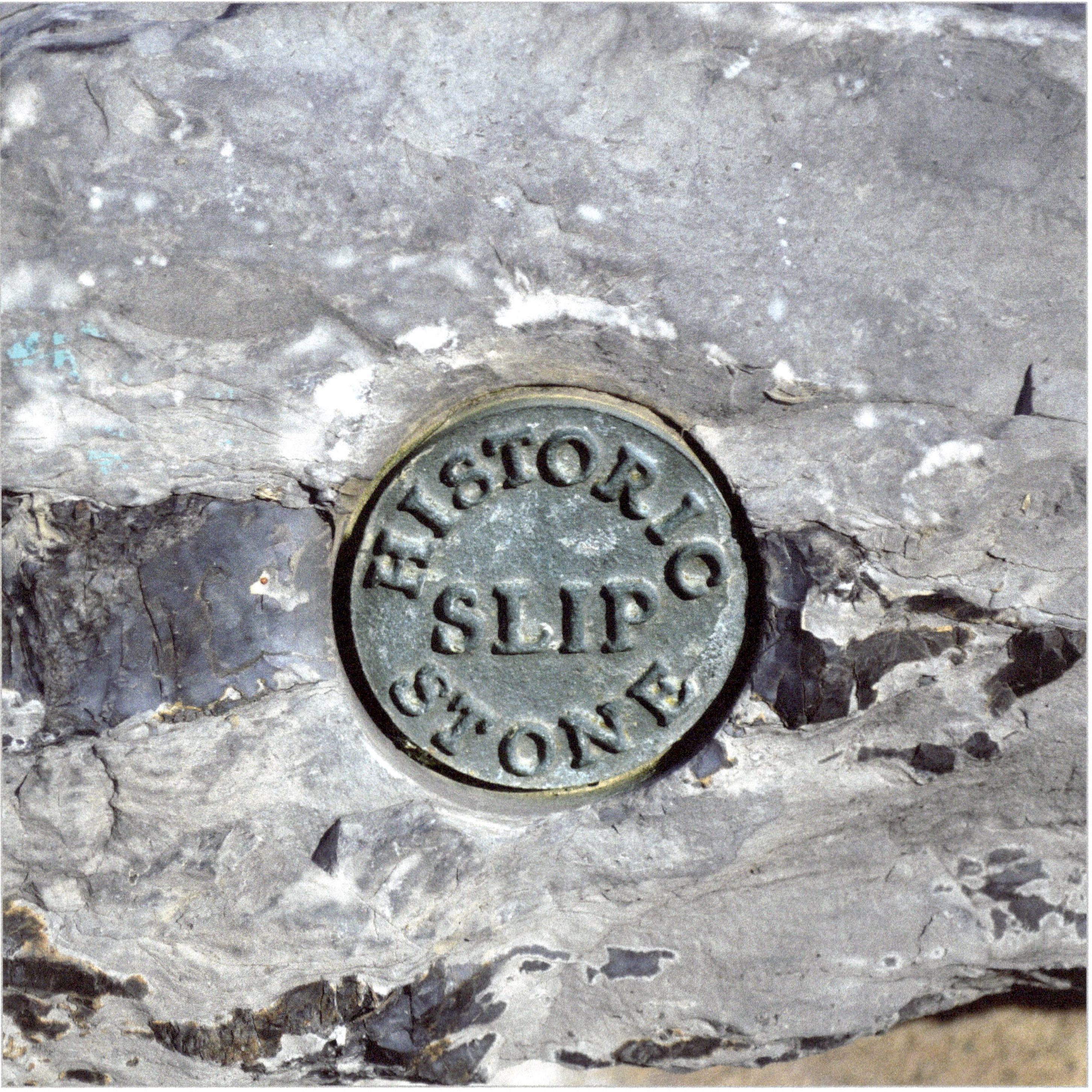

HISTORIC
SLIP
STONE

# Where history explodes

Socially and historically, the terminus of the Erie Canal was the most valuable real estate in Buffalo, bringing a huge injection of wealth from the commerce that changed hands here. It was a magnet that attracted the best and brightest to Buffalo and literally built this city. It was right here in 1825 where the canal opened and changed America. Buffalo was in precisely the right place at the right time.

Branded Canalside, today this space is Ground Zero for the renaissance of our city. Now that it is excavated, rewatered and the ruins of some historic buildings and cobblestone streets are exposed, both tourists and residents flock here. Retaining our history and giving people access to the beauty of our inner harbor is an ever growing success. It's almost unimaginable that this scenario nearly failed to happen.

In 1999, over the passionate outcry of preservationists, New York State was hell-bent on ignoring the significance of this historic spot and barreling ahead with generic boat slips and a landscaping plan. During the excavation the stone walls of the western terminus were uncovered. Struggling for any excuse to respond to the now deafening drum-beat of the public, state officials made an absolutely bizarre claim. If uncovered, the canal stones would "explode" in the winter's freeze-thaw cycle.

Thanks to a pair of UB geologists who volunteered to perform independent tests, the argument for not unearthing history was summarily debunked. People-power prevailed. A series of citizen-driven forums and public meetings eventually created the master plan to save this vital slice of Buffalo history.

Hidden to all but boaters, a few silver dollar-size brass plaques identifying the historic slip stone adorn the walls of the canal terminus.

**25**

**Banks of the Erie Canal Terminus**
Canalside, Buffalo, NY 14203

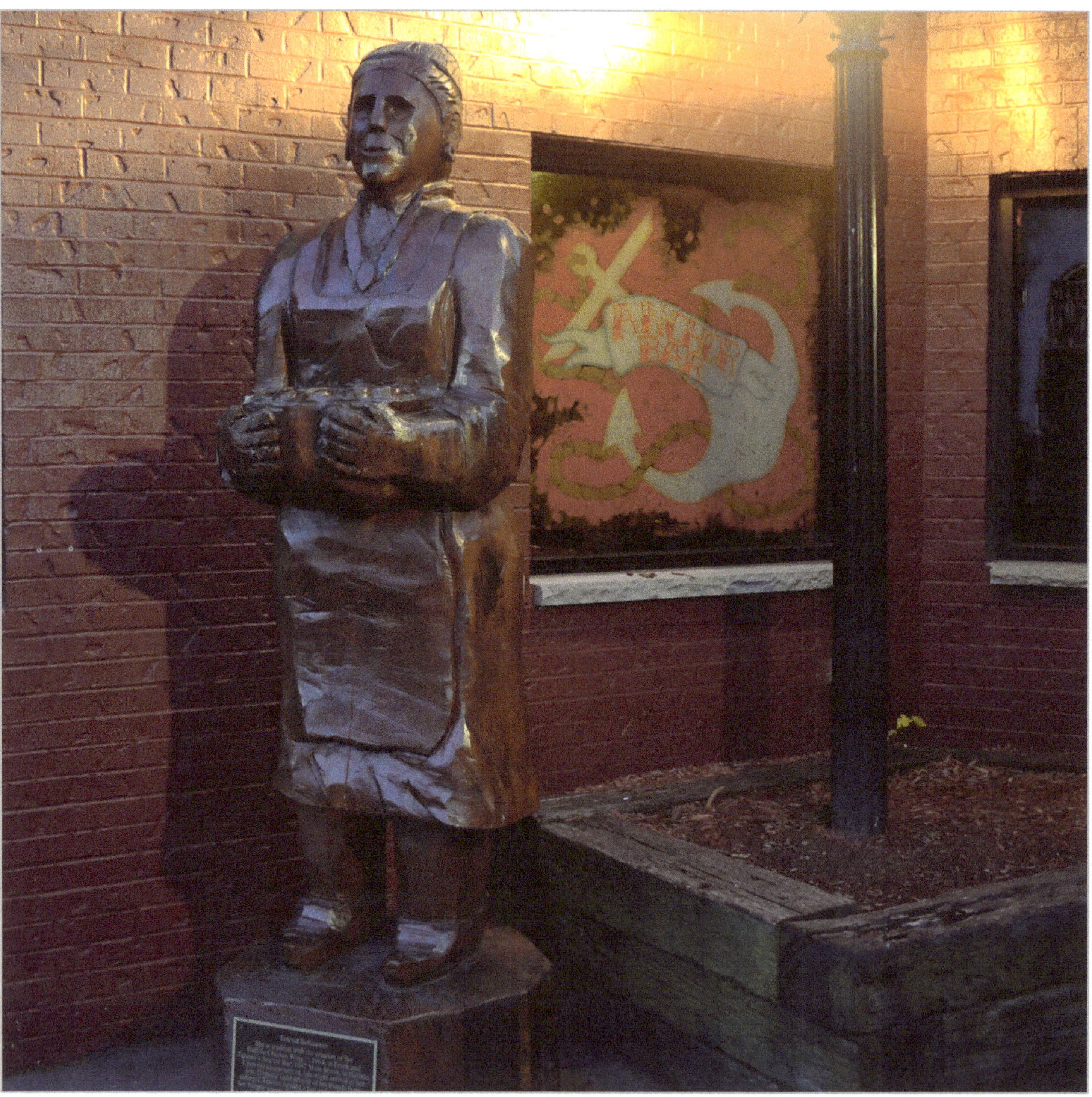

# Winging it

As every chicken knows, Teressa Bellissimo did not invent chicken wings. She is, however, credited with being the first to deep-fry them and cover them with hot sauce. She created a world-wide bar food sensation with something that normally would have been thrown away.

Carvings for a Cause takes trees downed by storms that normally would have been thrown away and transforms them into works of art. They are sculpted to look like people who have played important roles in Western New York history.

Therese Forton-Barnes' inspirational idea came from a rare October 2006 storm in which more than 40,000 trees were destroyed. The project has not only benefited Buffalo by leaving an art trail of nearly forty amazing carvings in its wake, but has also raised funds for community tree-planting efforts. The wooden sculptures have literally created a home-grown connective tissue throughout the city.

Teressa Bellissimo, shown here, is carved from a 100-year-old silver maple. The wooden wings she is serving are perfect fare for those on a high fiber diet.

**26**

**Frank and Teressa's Anchor Bar**
1047 Main Street, Buffalo, NY 14209

# Flight path

One of the most iconic sculptures in the city is "Birds Excited Into Flight" on Bidwell Parkway created by Larry W. Griffis Jr. (1924-2000). A prolific artist, Griffis also designed "Spirit of Womanhood" along the Scajaquada Expressway, and founded Griffis Sculpture Park, a 400-acre nature preserve with 225 monumental sculptures located in Ashford Hollow, NY, south of Buffalo.

"Birds Excited Into Flight" dramatically depicts seven human figures standing in a circle with their upraised arms evolving into stylized birds taking to the sky. It is a twenty-feet-high, cold-rolled steel work completed in 1981.

This project almost didn't happen. Griffis installations had a long history of being a magnet for bureaucratic confrontations. One of the more celebrated of these dust-ups came during the summer of 1980, when a hue and cry was heard from then Buffalo Mayor James Griffin, who had construction halted on "Birds Excited Into Flight." Hizzoner felt that Griffis and his colleagues had not obtained the proper municipal blessing to begin the work. Fortunately for the city and future generations, cooler heads eventually prevailed and the project moved forward.

Bidwell Parkway is part of the Buffalo's Olmsted Park System, the nation's first park and parkway system.  This living masterpiece was designed by the pre-eminent landscape architects Calvert Vaux and Frederick Law Olmsted. The word "parkway" was actually coined in their proposal for Central Park, and improved upon with their plan for the Buffalo Park System.  The parkways extend long green fingers throughout the city, punctuated by beautifully landscaped traffic circles which link six major Olmsted parks.

27

**"Birds Excited Into Flight," by Larry Griffis Jr.**
Bidwell Parkway between Elmwood and Potomac, Buffalo, NY 14222

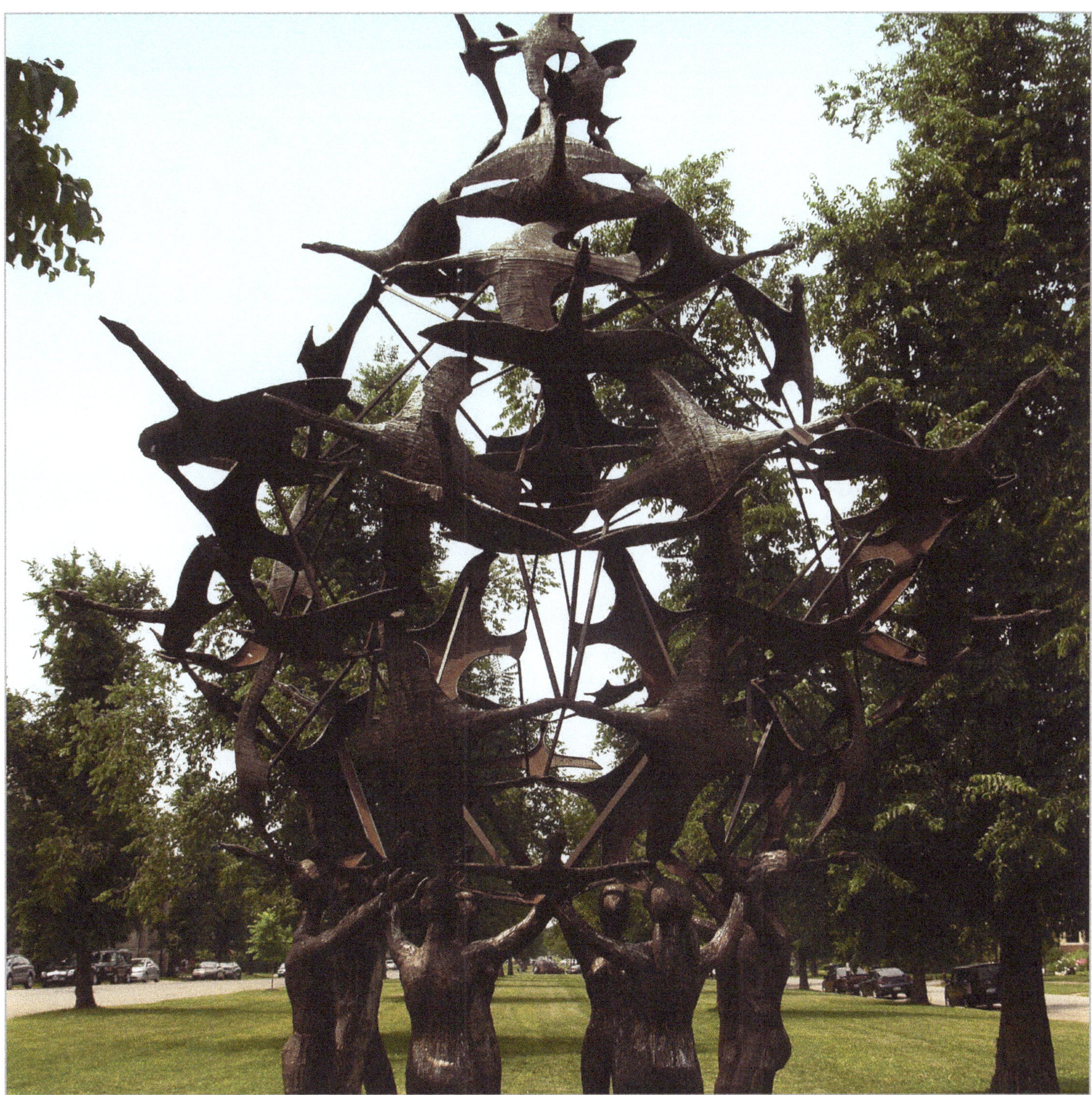

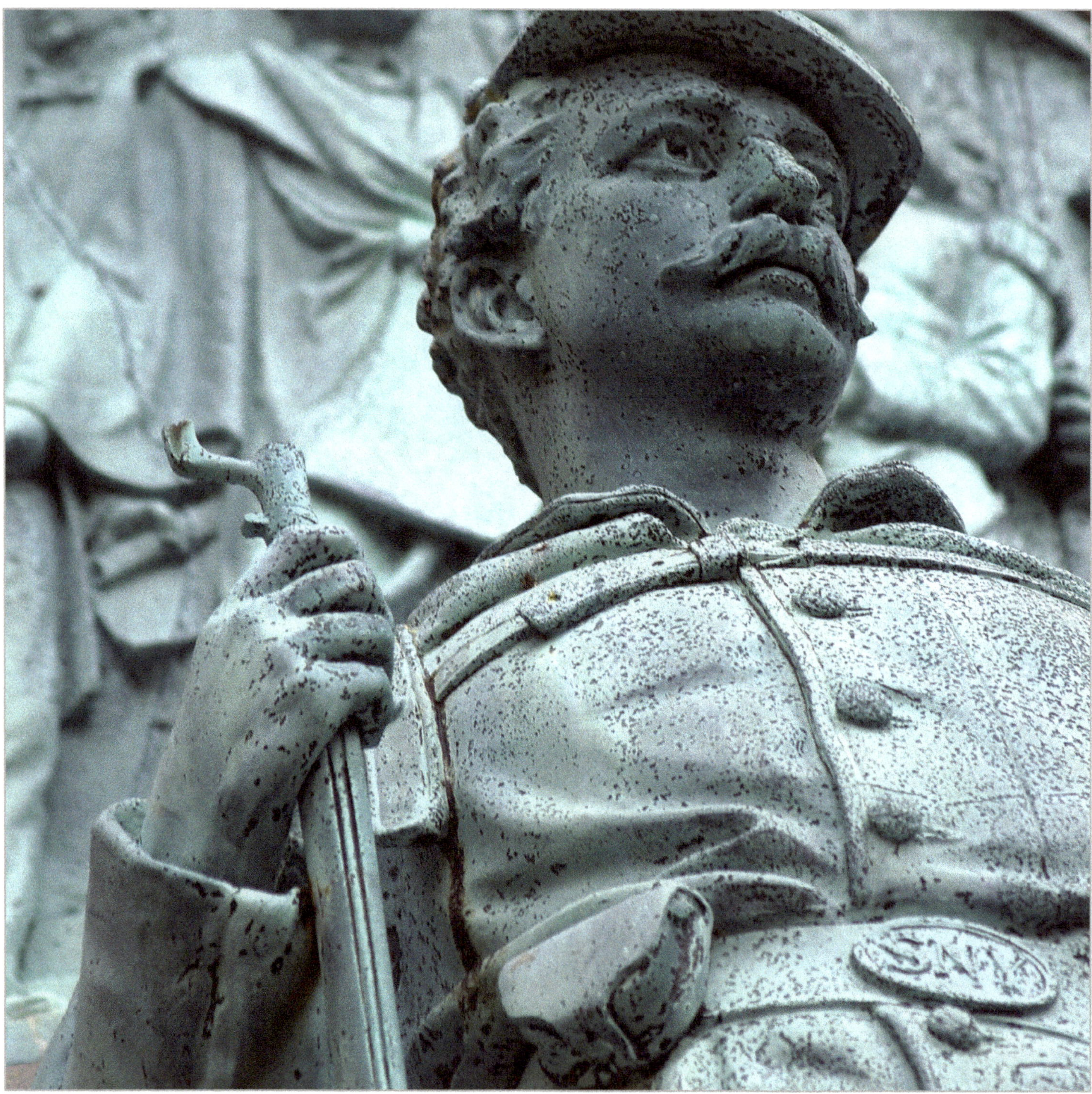

# Party animal

If there's a city-wide celebration in Buffalo, odds are it's happening in Lafayette Square. Throughout our history, the space where Main, Broadway, Washington, and Court streets meet has been the city's heart, soul, and party headquarters. In the past, Lafayette Square has been host to audiences for such luminaries as Henry Clay, Daniel Webster, Abraham Lincoln, and every garage band in the region. From 1986 to 2011, it was home to a free concert series known as Thursday at the Square.

The square was named for Marie-Joseph-Paul-Yves-Roch-Gilbert du Motier, Marquis de Lafayette (or as his close friends called him, General Lafayette) who visited Buffalo in 1825. Its center is dominated by the Soldiers and Sailors monument. An eighty-four-feet marble column is surrounded by four bronze statues representing the infantry, cavalry, artillery, and navy, topped by a mysterious crown-wearing woman holding a sword, shield, and laurel wreath. It was sculpted by Caspar Buberl, an artist whose portfolio includes Civil War statues, Civil War statues, and more Civil War statues.

Soldiers and Sailors monument has a rather topsy-turvy history. It was dedicated on July 4, 1884, with great pomp and circumstance including a full gaggle of generals and politicians, Masonic ritual, parades, horse races, and fireworks. Just five years later in 1889, the monument had to be rebuilt as it had already begun to lean and was considered unsafe. Even the 1882 "time capsule" beneath it had been crushed and its contents destroyed by water. Costing nearly as much to fix as it did to build, the monument emerged nearly fifteen feet taller.

But, the memorial's storied history doesn't end there. In 1973, a vehicle driven by an unlicensed driver with the unlikely name of Darrell Penis jumped the curb and struck the monument. Penis was convicted of driving under the influence. And as recently as 1982, the Niagara Frontier Transit Authority (unsuccessfully) asked that the monument be demolished or reconstructed at another location.

**28**

**"Soldiers and Sailors Monument," by Caspar Buberl**
Lafayette Square, Buffalo, NY 14202

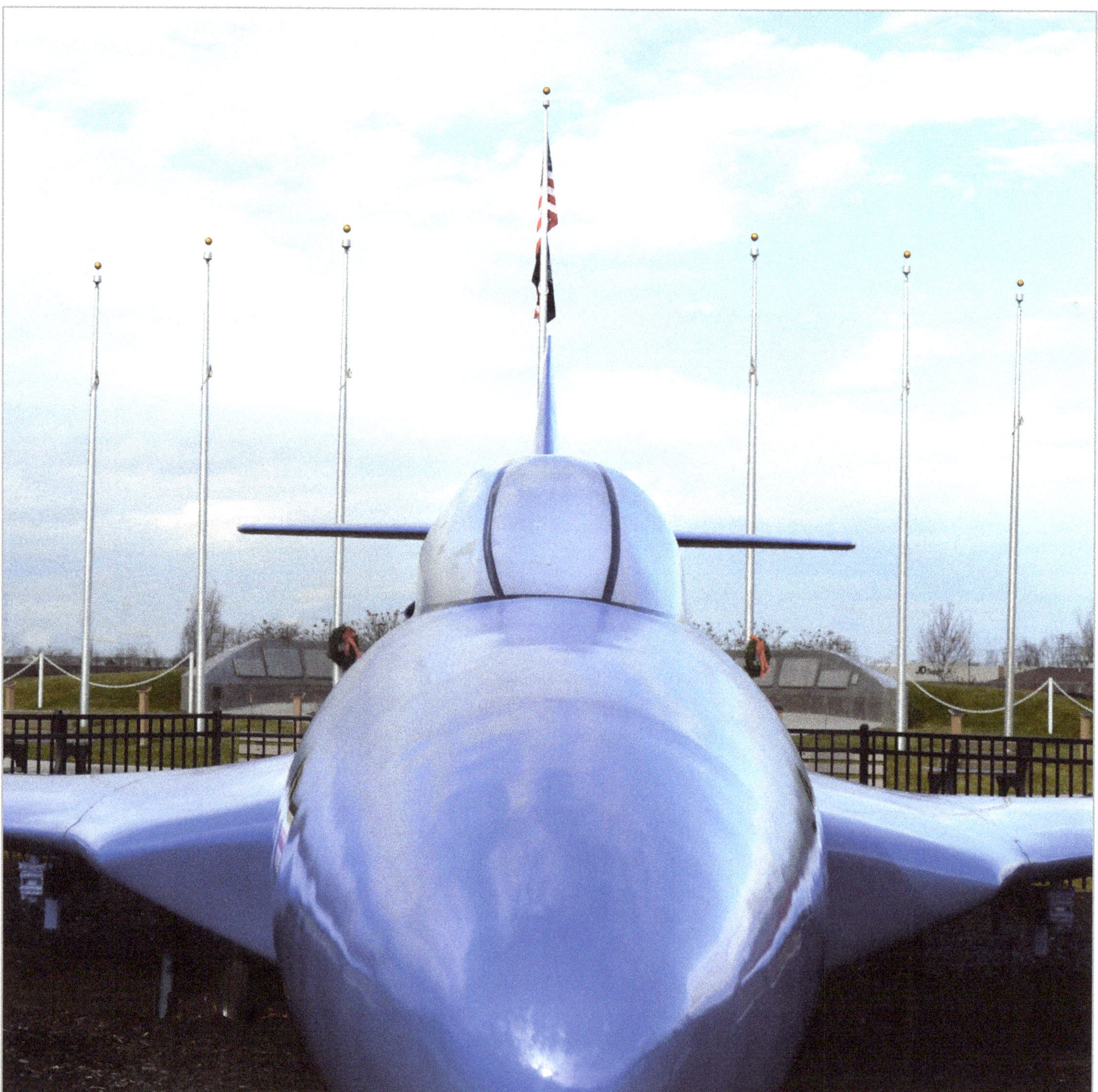

# Way below the radar

Since May 1959, the "blue jet" has diligently defended the southeast portion of Walter M. Kenney field in the Town of Tonawanda at the corner of Colvin and Brighton avenues. The Korean War-era Grumman F9F-6P Cougar Naval airframe is on loan from the National Museum of Naval Aviation.

The blue jet will be remembered as the ultimate piece of playground equipment by generations of children. For nearly 50 years, climbing on the plane's wings or straddling the fuselage was never actively discouraged by the town.

For the slightly older kids, shimmying up the vertical stabilizer and sitting on the tail was an unspoken right of passage. Really old former kids can even recall a time when they could crawl through the tail of the plane and sit in the cockpit for a role-playing experience that could never be replicated by any military recruitment effort.

Cosmetically repaired and repainted as a volunteer effort by a local auto collision business, the blue jet is now the cornerstone of a Town of Tonawanda Veterans Memorial dedicated in August 2009 by General and former Secretary of State Colin Powell. A four-feet high black wrought-iron fence forms a pentagon around the jet, keeping eager climbers off and upholding the town's new agreement with the US Government to protect it.

**29**

**Town of Tonawanda Veterans Memorial - Walter M. Kenney Field**
Brighton Road at Colvin Boulevard. Town of Tonawanda, NY 14150

# A chip off the ole Rock Pile

So much has happened in this space on Jefferson Avenue. Long before it was Johnnie B. Wiley Athletic Field, this relatively unassuming chunk of East-side real estate at Best and Jefferson had been used for a staggering array of purposes.

It was originally the site of the Prospect Reservoir. Buffalo relied on the reservoir for water pressure until the Colonel Ward Pumping Plant was built in 1915. No longer in use, the construction of a single tier grandstand stadium began in 1935 as part of President Franklin Roosevelt's WPA make-work program. The joke of the day was that more people helped build the stadium than the Pyramids.

Since it opened in 1938, the stadium has had almost as many names as eskimo have for snow. It was originally named after Charles E. Roesch, mayor of Buffalo. A few months later the name was changed to Grover Cleveland Stadium, and then to Civic Stadium a few months after that. In 1960, it received its final name of War Memorial Stadium.

The city hadn't really planned to have a stadium, so uses for this new facility were pretty much invented as they went along. Initially used just for special events, it evolved into a venue for midget racing and eventually NASCAR. Richard Petty made his debut here. It hosted the original AAFC Buffalo Bills from 1946-1949 and the AFL/NFL Bills of today from 1960-1972. It was also home to Bison baseball on and off from 1961to 1987, as well as Canisius College's baseball and football teams. In 1983-84, the movie "The Natural" starring Robert Redford was filmed here.

With the construction of Rich Stadium (now Ralph Wilson Stadium) in Orchard Park and Pilot Field (now Coca-Cola Field) in downtown Buffalo, the aging stadium was demolished in 1988. Only the iconic entrance featuring a relief carving of a Buffalo still remains. Today it is the site of an athletic facility used by Buffalo Public schools' athletic teams, youth football and baseball leagues, and other special events.

**30**

**Johnnie B. Wiley Athletic Field - Entrance**
285 Dodge Street at Jefferson, Buffalo, NY 14208

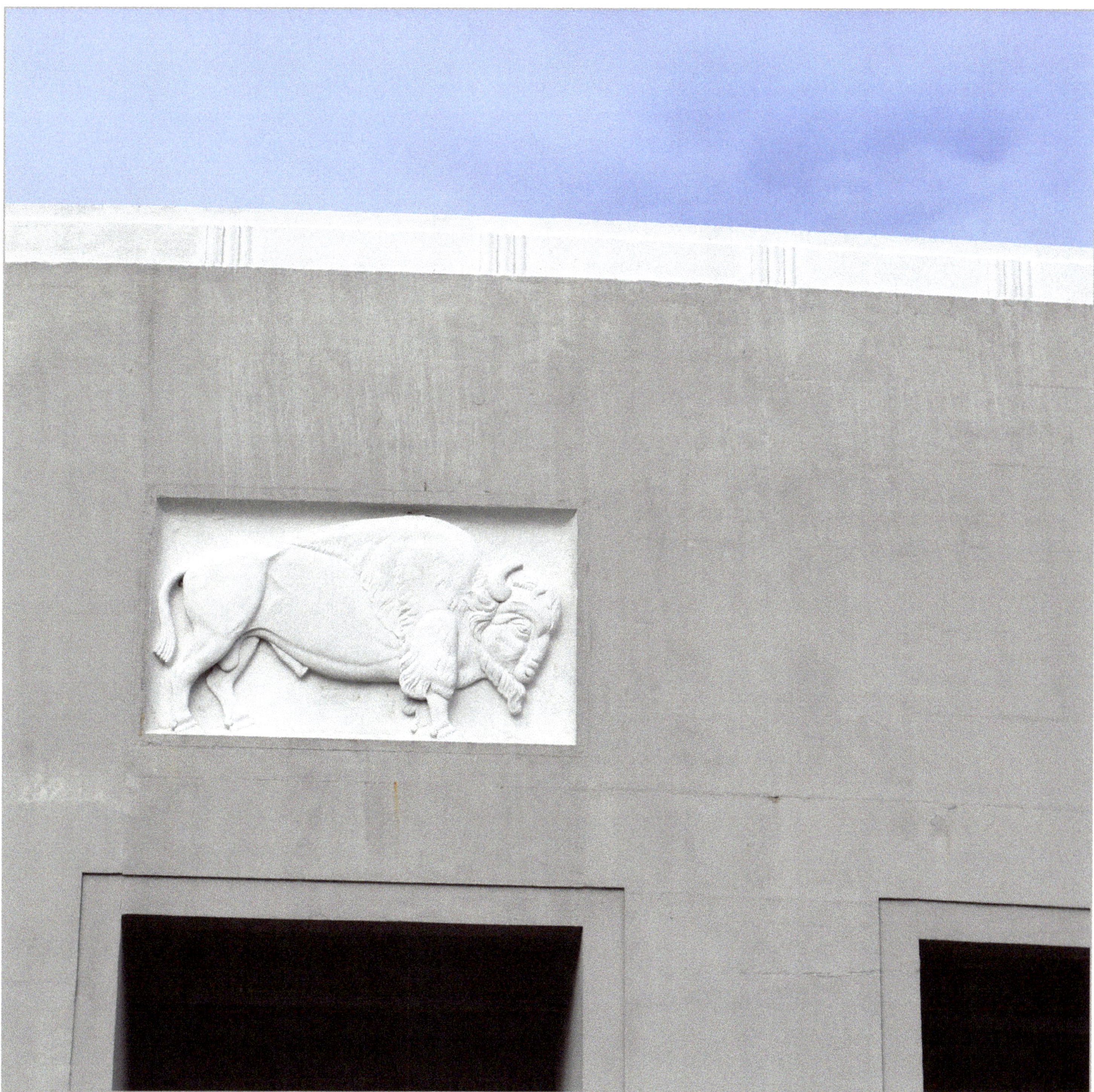

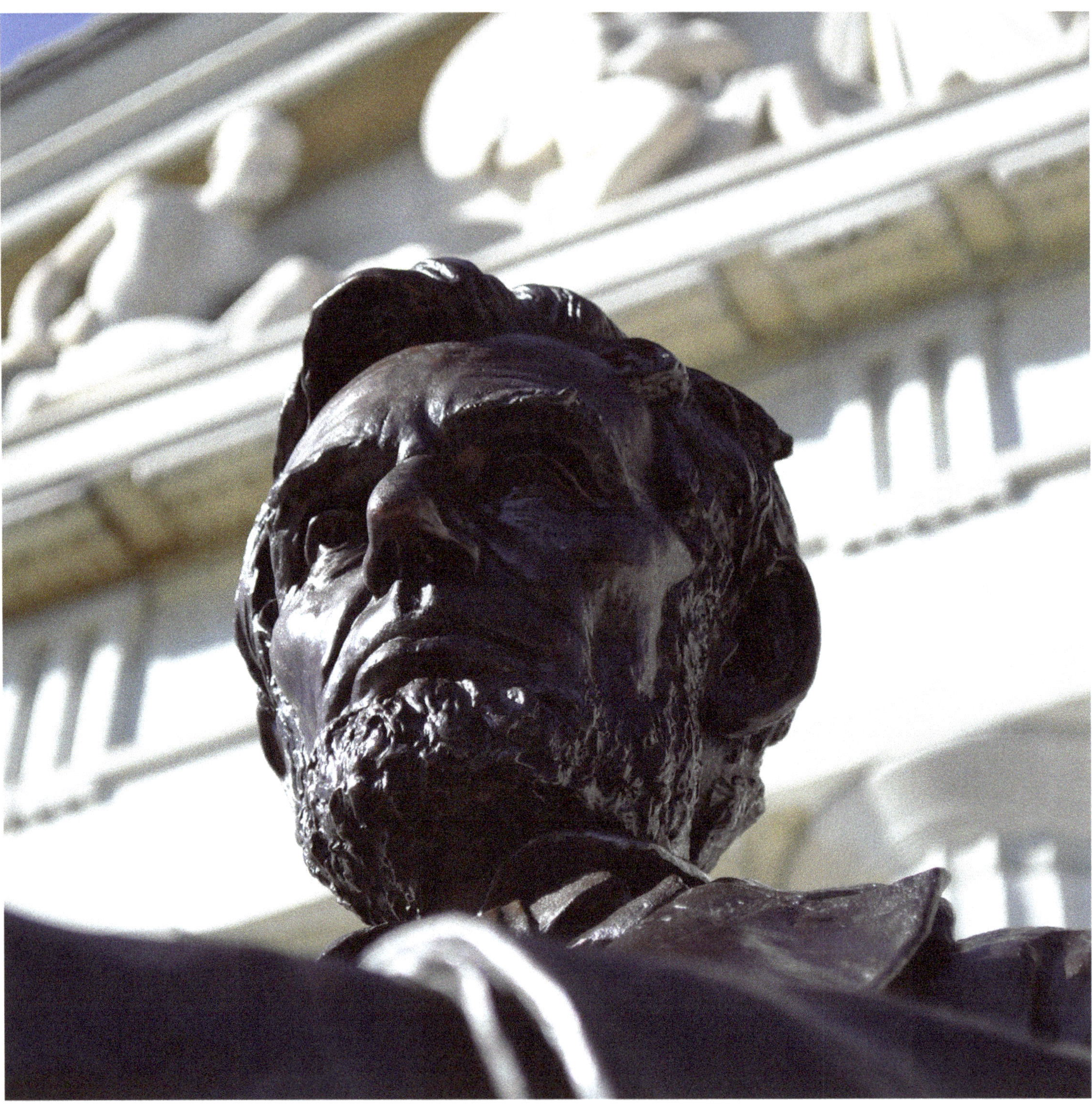

# Happy Birthday, Abe

The Lincoln Statue on the South Portico of the The Buffalo History Museum is a tribute to Mr. Lincoln and the passion of Buffalo druggist Julius Francis.

Following the assassination of President Abraham Lincoln, Francis, who quite possibly was the original "Log Cabin Republican," became determined to preserve and promote the martyred President's memory. He amassed a large collection of Civil War and Lincoln memorabilia, but his main goal was to create a national observance of Lincoln's birthday, February 12.

His two attempts to persuade Congress to establish a national Lincoln's Birthday holiday failed. Francis died in 1881, having founded the Buffalo Lincoln's Birthday Association, which continued the work.

In his will, Francis, who was a bachelor, made the Association the sole heir to his estate. Using the funds he left, the Association commissioned sculptor Charles H. Niehaus to create a statue of Lincoln. The statue's original location was in an area of the new Buffalo Historical Society building appropriately named "The Lincoln Room," which also contained the Francis Lincoln memorabilia collection.

In the early 1930s, the statue was moved outdoors to the South Portico where it remains today. The memorabilia, which includes Abraham Lincoln's Life Mask and Hands, created in plaster by Leonard Volk two days after Lincoln was nominated for President, remains one of the Museum's most celebrated collections. Lincoln's right hand was still swollen from shaking hands with supporters.

**"Lincoln, the Emancipator," by Charles H. Niehaus**
The Buffalo History Museum
One Museum Court, Buffalo, NY 14216

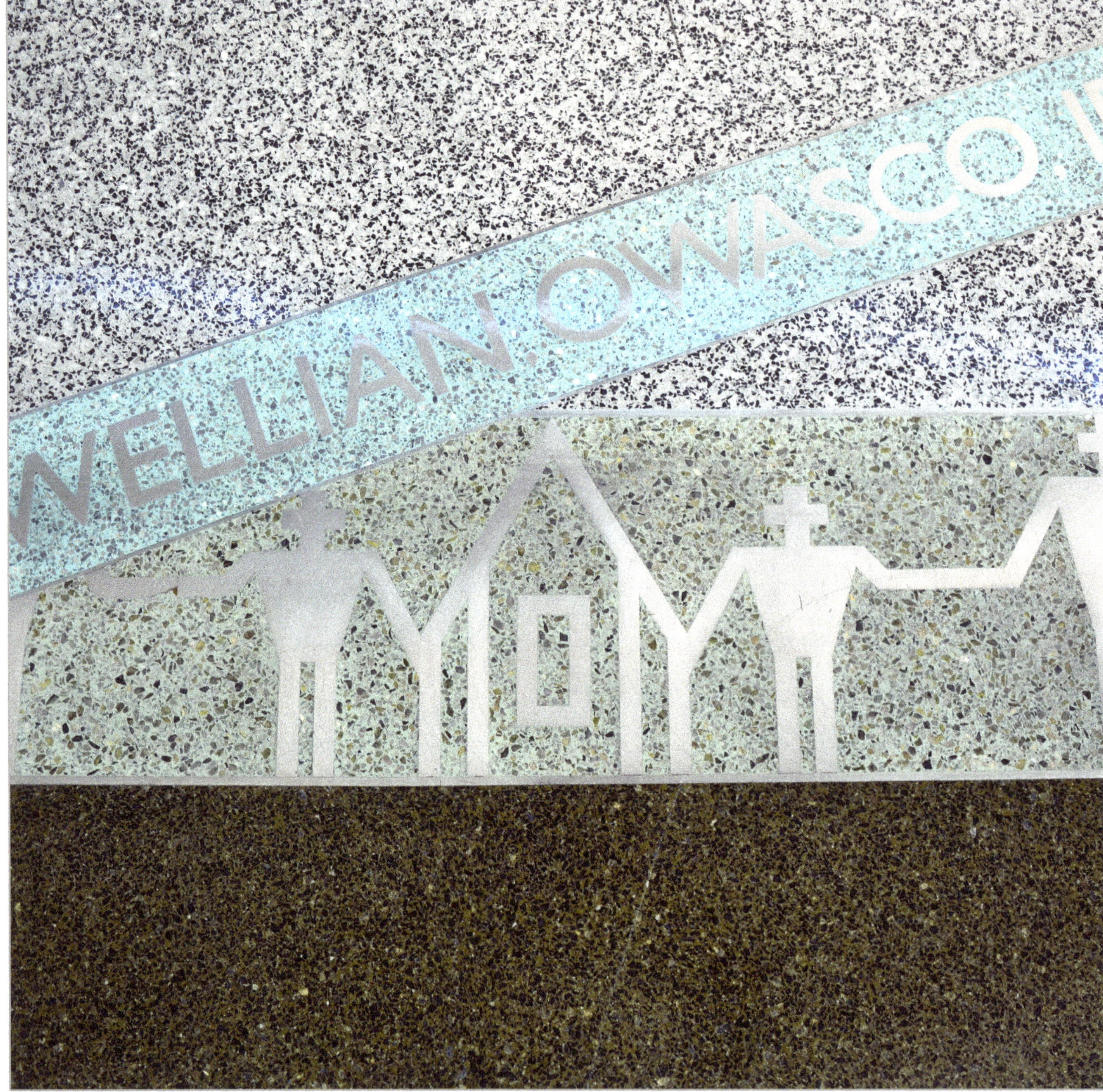
MELLIAN, OWASCO.

# Take off your shoes and fly

When you go to the airport, before you go up, look down. In addition to standing in long lines, removing your footwear, and being groped by strangers, be sure to check out some of the public art.

After all, you'll be standing on it.

Buffalo Niagara International Airport is home to a 13,000-square-feet terrazzo floor design created by Robert Calvo. A series of eight thematic paths meander through this Niagara Frontier Transit Authority (NFTA) property, each representing a slice of Buffalo Niagara's development, from the prehistoric to the present. At some points the interconnected pattern of colored tile strands are as wide as sixty-five feet.

The NFTA has a long history of presenting a rich visual landscape within its facilities. Curated by Buffalo art dealer Nina Freudenheim in 1985, the public art projects in the Buffalo Niagara Metro Rail system have brought contemporary art to every subway station along Main Street. That project is said to have cost $1.15 million.

**32**

**Buffalo Niagara International Airport - Main Concourse**
4200 Genesee Street, Cheektowaga, NY 14225

# A sleeping woman

After attending the 1901 Pan-American Exposition in Buffalo, there were those who believed they had seen it all. The world had nothing left to give.

> *"A few more Expositions and we shall have left nothing that is wonderfully, wonderful, nothing superlatively, strange, and the delicious word foreign will have dropped out of the language. Where shall we go to get us a new sensation?"*
>
> *- Mary Bronson Hartt from her essay "The Play Side Of The Fair"*

Go to the Buffalo Historical Society's Resource Center to begin to grasp what Ms. Bronson Hartt meant. The entrance is a thirty-five-feet tall replica of the lady's head that graced the façade of a 1901 Pan-Am midway attraction called "Dreamland."  She is wearing pearls the size of bowling balls, and you entered the more than 100-year old trolley barn into the Exposition Hall through her cleavage.

The "Dreamland" ride consisted of a mirror maze. It was said that "No illusion on the Midway is more confusing or amusing."

The Midway occupied nearly a third of the Exposition and contained more than forty exhibits.

**33**

**The Buffalo History Museum Resource Center**
459 Forest Avenue, Buffalo, NY 14213

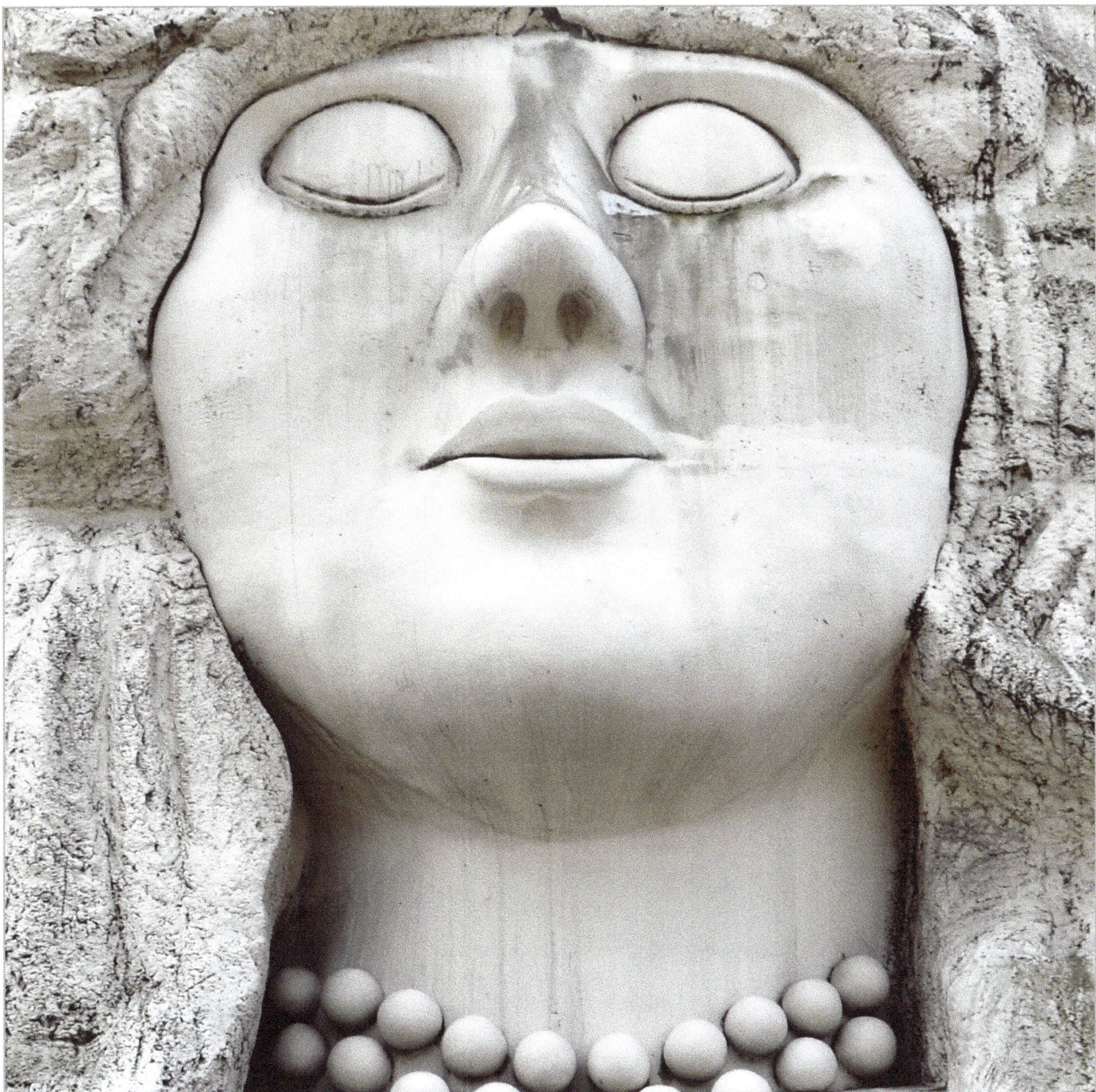

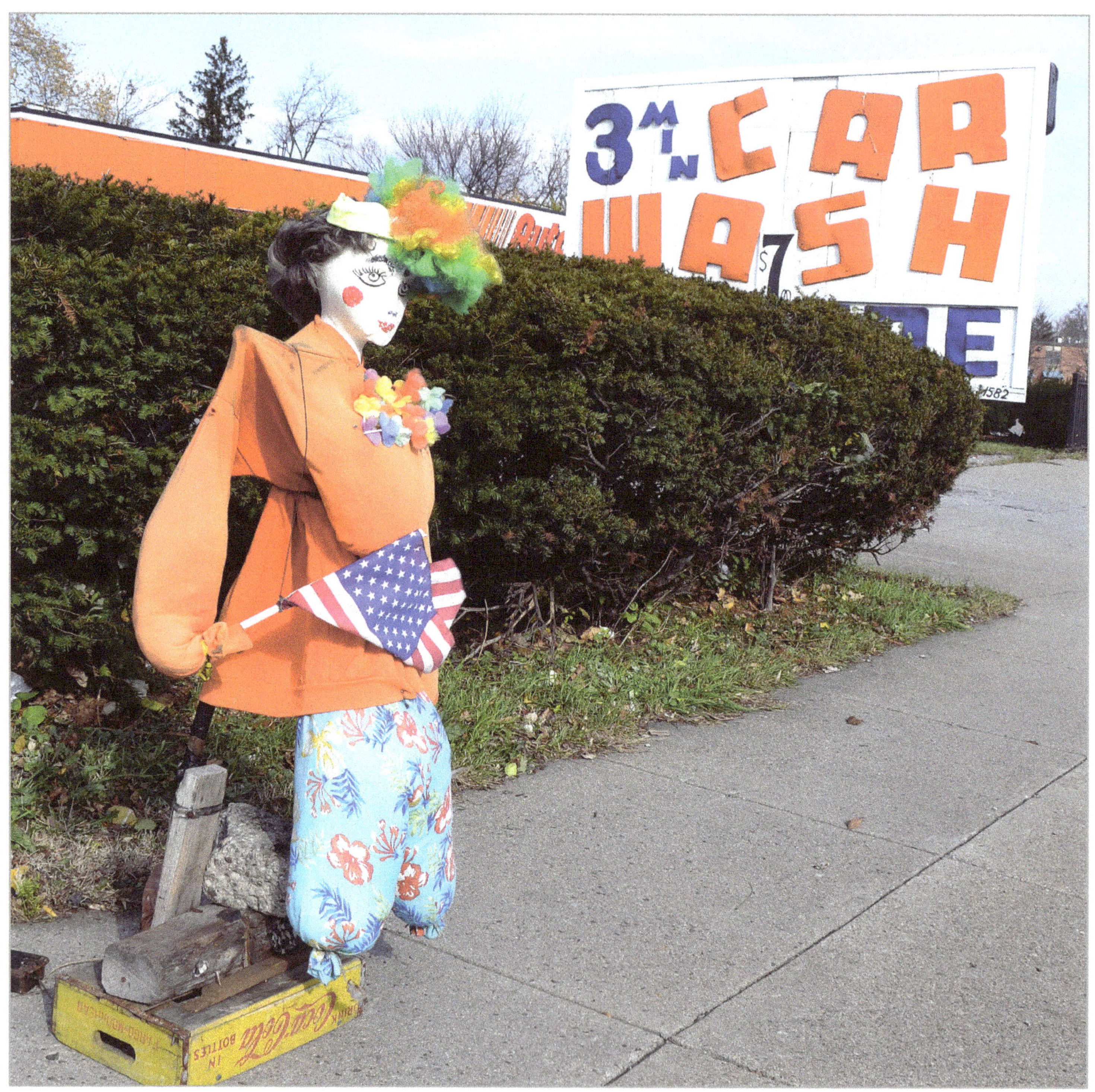

3 MIN CAR
WASH
$7
4582
Drink Coca-Cola
IN LARGE KING-SIZE BOTTLES

# Anything can happen at the car wash

As any savvy marketer will tell you, sex sells.  It's the foundation of advertising for most perfumes, apparel, and luxury automobile ads. In Buffalo, an inventive entrepreneur has extended this concept to the automotive exterior maintenance market.

Meet Estelle, the spokes-model for the 3-Minute Car Wash on Main Street.  She's been luring customers into the facility to have their vehicles cleaned since the mid-1970s.

Every day, through rain, shine, and all the rest of the weather Western New York is famous for, she suggestively poses between the sidewalk and the curb shaking every inch of her girlish charm. Curiously enough, the harder the wind blows, the more flirtatiously she shimmies.

Capturing the imagination of the thousands of drivers who whiz by everyday is no easy task on this hotly competitive urban art block. Estelle goes toe-to-toe daily with a car that's plunging through a second floor wall across the street and a shiny motorcycle on the roof of a building on the very next corner.

During her more than forty-year career, a milestone literally unheard of within the modeling industry, Estelle has always managed to keep fit and trim, even when Freddies Doughnuts was open across the street.

What a looker.

**34**

**"Estelle"**
Main Automatic Car Wash Inc.
1582 Main Street, Buffalo, NY 14209

# Generally absent

Even through the blurry lens of war, Union General Philip Henry Sheridan was not a very nice guy.

A ruthless warrior during the Civil War, many believe General Sheridan should be considered a war criminal. In 1864, after the retreating Confederate Army had been thoroughly routed from Virginia's Shenandoah Valley, Sheridan ordered his 35,000 infantry troops to burn and kill virtually everything in sight, leaving innocent women and children utterly destitute without shelter in winter, without food, or any means of growing crops or livestock with which to feed themselves. Looking over the scorched earth he left behind, Sheridan boasted, "A crow flying over must carry its own provisions."

After the war Sheridan was appointed overseer of the Indian Territory where he supervised the genocide of Native Americans. He is famous for coining the phrase, "The only good Indian is a dead Indian."

Countless cities have large bronze statues standing in his honor. The Town of Tonawanda has a large marble statue base honoring Sheridan – but it does not memorialize the General, but rather fashionable Sheridan Road in Chicago.

An equestrian statue of the General atop the base was briefly considered in 1925, but the project was cancelled and installed instead in Albany in front of the New York State Capitol where it still stands today.

**35**

**Sheridan Monument**
Sheridan Drive near Delaware Avenue, Town of Tonawanda, NY 14150

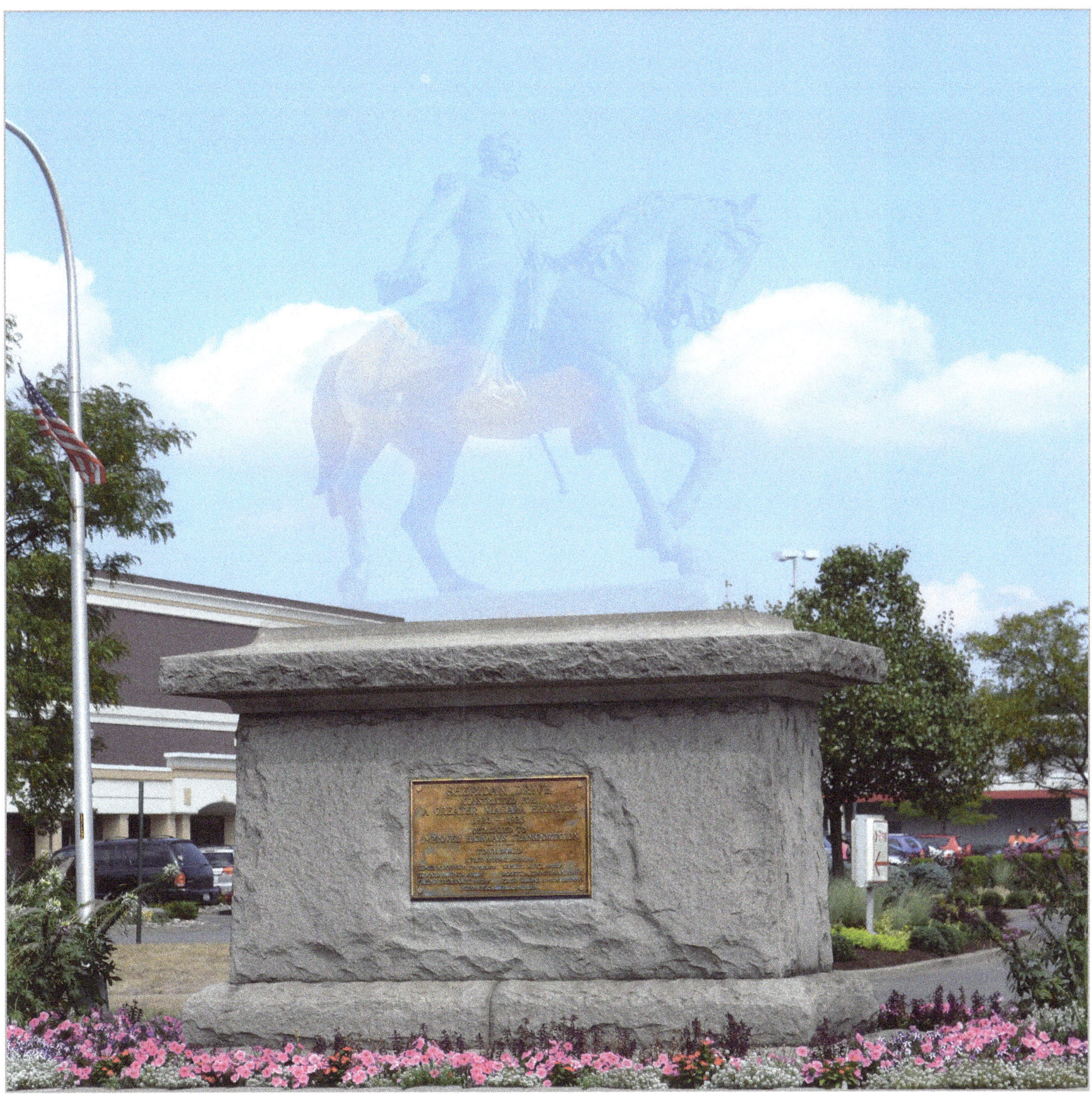

# Dancing in the streets

Buffalo's Elmwood Strip, with its unique blend of shops, galleries, nightclubs, bars, and restaurants, has always had a special glow and rhythm. In the early 1980s this aura became much more defined. The glow became a distinctive deep-blue neon, and the beat a very sassy tango.

Commissioned by the Buffalo Department of Community Development, the city needed a community lighting solution. They were originally thinking along the lines of a row of Victorian-style street lights. By coloring just a bit outside the lines, Dan Sack, an artistic technical consultant, Laura Rankin, a graphic illustrator, and Andy Ferullo, a filmmaker, pushed the initiative in a rather unexpected direction. Through a bit of research, some shoe-leather consensus building, and a modern twist on a 1920s technology, they were able to connect the dots of the commercial district and transform it into a cohesive "Blue Light District."

This public/private partnership, funded with what amounts to the change in the couch by city project standards, unleashed a 1,200 feet ribbon of blue neon to stripe the facades of no fewer than fifty-nine businesses. The result was an elegant solution, visually bonding a six-block area. This was anchored by a mesmerizing neon billboard at the southern end of the project, featuring a couple gracefully tangoing across its twenty-feet expanse. Some ground-breaking electronic transitioning helped to create this fabulous illusion.

There is an important lesson to be learned from this project. If you assign a mundane task to a group of highly creative people, be prepared for a little magic.

37

"**Tango Dancers,**" © by Laura Rankin, Dan Sack, and Andy Ferullo
976 Elmwood Avenue, Buffalo, NY 14222

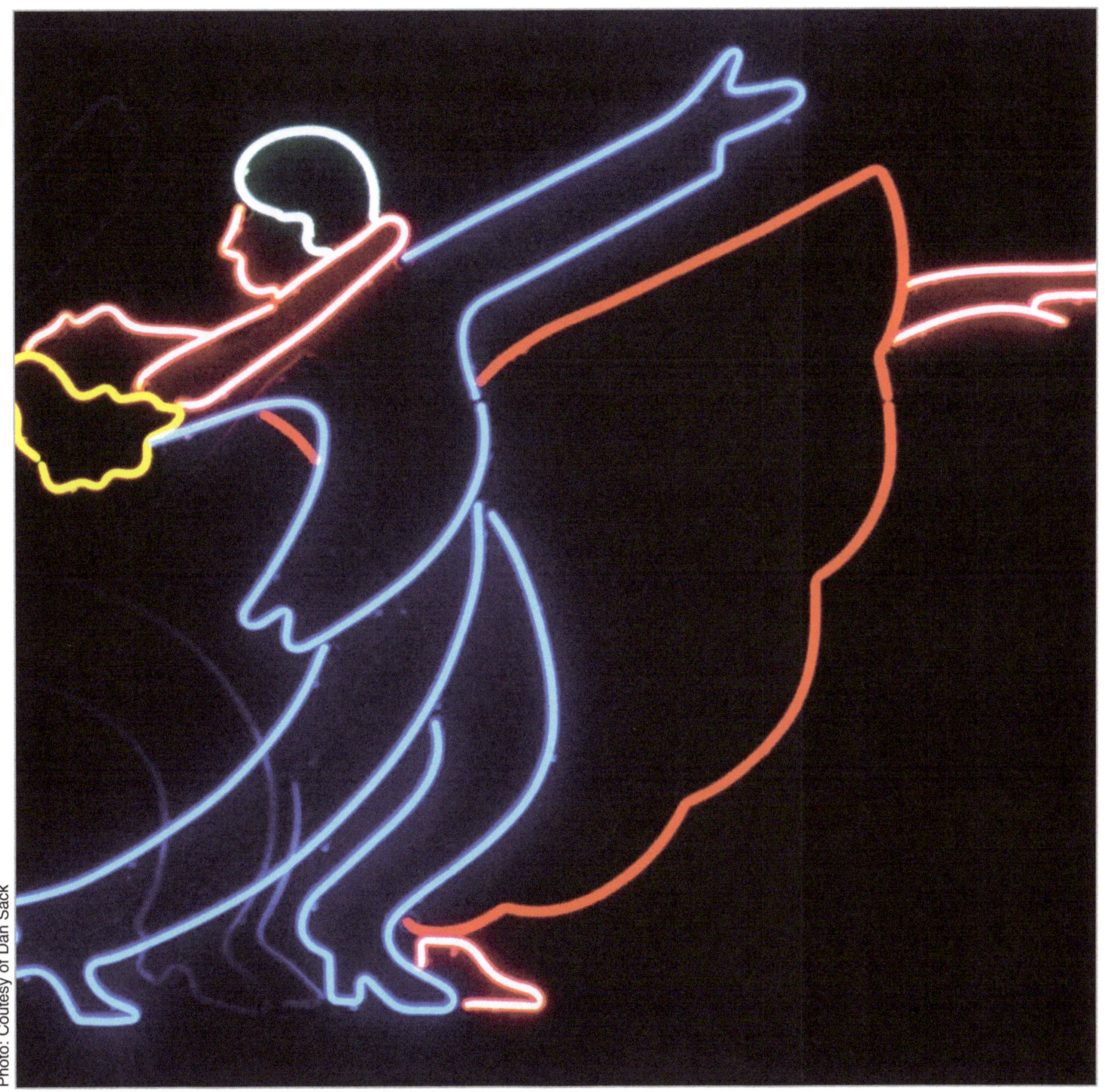

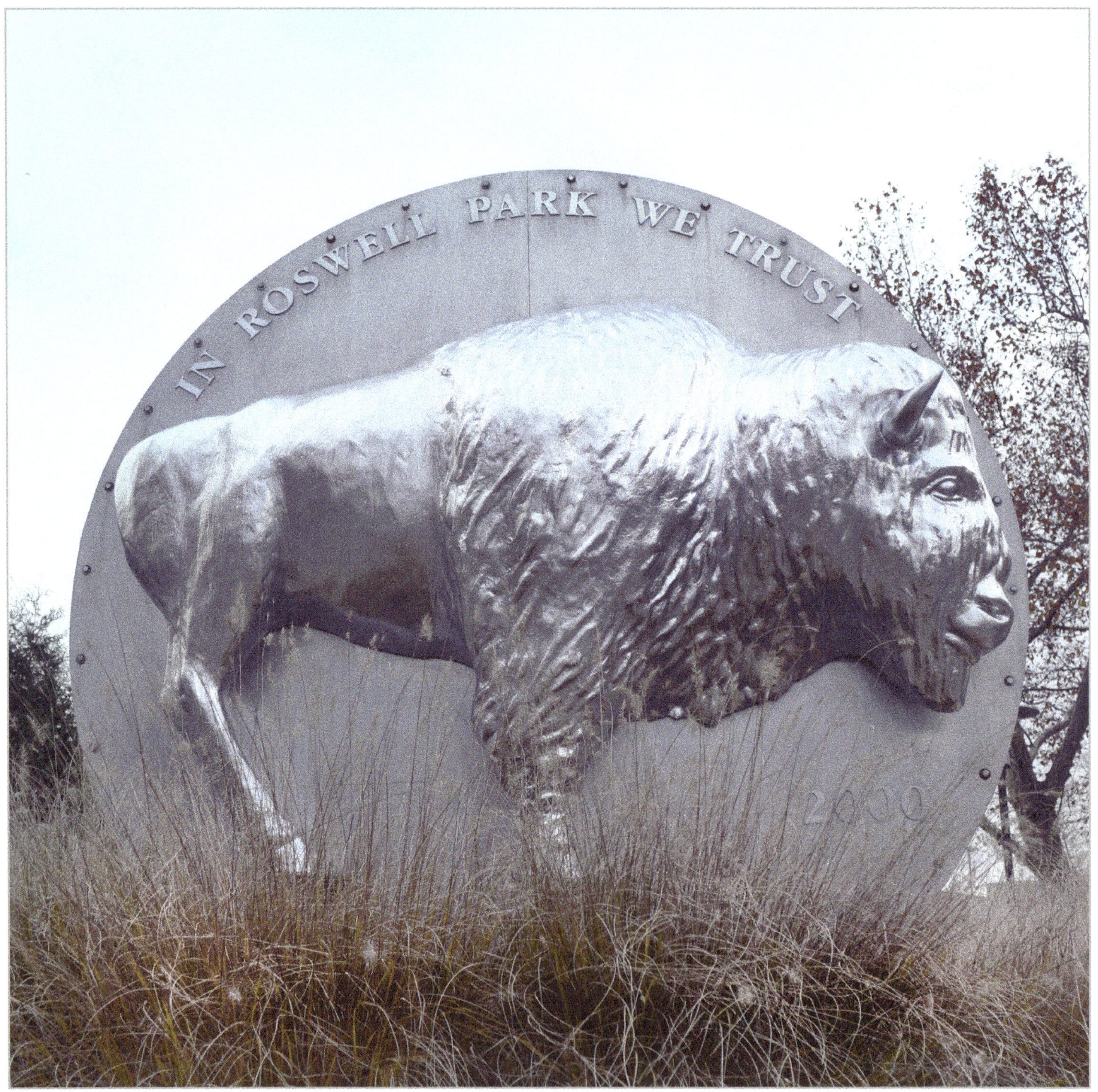

IN ROSWELL PARK WE TRUST
2000

# Raising nickels in the Nickel City

Herd About Buffalo was a public art project and fundraiser that roamed Buffalo's streets during the summer of 2000. It was conceived and inspired by Roswell Park Cancer Institute volunteer Patty Capstraw Wilkins, who was facing her own health challenges at that time. Sadly, she lost her battle with brain cancer before the project's completion.

The program unleashed a stampede of more than 150 life-sized fiberglass buffalo statues that grazed the streets to raise funds for cancer research and patient care at Roswell Park Cancer Institute and continuing art education programs at the Burchfield Penney Art Center.

Painted and decorated by local artists, Herd About Buffalo was a brilliant way to raise $1.6 million for a good cause while simultaneously decorating the city.

More than a decade later the buffalo are still sighted around town. They've recently been spotted attending Williamsville South High School, grazing in front of Bing's Restaurant, visiting their attorney in the Brisbane Building, and on the roof of Cole's, one of their favorite watering holes.

**38**

**Herd About Buffalo**
Roswell Park Cancer Institute
Carlton and Elm Streets, Buffalo, NY 14203

# Well connected

It's October 12, 2012, opening weekend for the year's pandemic of Sabres fever as the team was scheduled to host the Pittsburgh Penguins. A crowd gathered in high anticipation on Alumni Plaza outside the First Niagara Center.

There was a noticeable gasp as fans first saw that only three players were wearing skates, the youngest of whom was born more than sixty years earlier. There had been murmers earlier about a labor dispute between the National Hockey League and the NHL Players' Association, which would put the season on hold.

However, that gasp was quickly replaced by a thunderous cheer as the form of the players came into focus. "The French Connection" are together again in Buffalo! Forty years after the celebrated forward line of Gilbert Perreault, Rene Robert and Rick Martin first skated together, the Sabres that night unveiled a seven-feet-high bronze statue honoring the trio.

Nicknamed after the film, with Perreault at center, Robert at right wing, and Martin at left wing, from 1972 to 1979 they combined to complete an amazing 1,116 goals and 2,573 total points in 2,396 games. This threesome is widely considered to be one of the greatest forward lines in NHL history.

Inspiration for the bronze statue came from a Ron Moscati photograph taken during the April 1975 playoff victory against the Montreal Canadiens. The Sabres commissioned distinguished American sculptor Jerry McKenna, renowned for his sports statues, to recapture the magic of the "The French Connection."

Plaques featuring the names of 401 Sabres alumni are also now on the Plaza.

39

**"The French Connection, " by Jerry McKenna**
First Niagara Center - Buffalo Sabres Alumni Plaza
One Seymour Knox III Plaza, Buffalo, NY, 14203

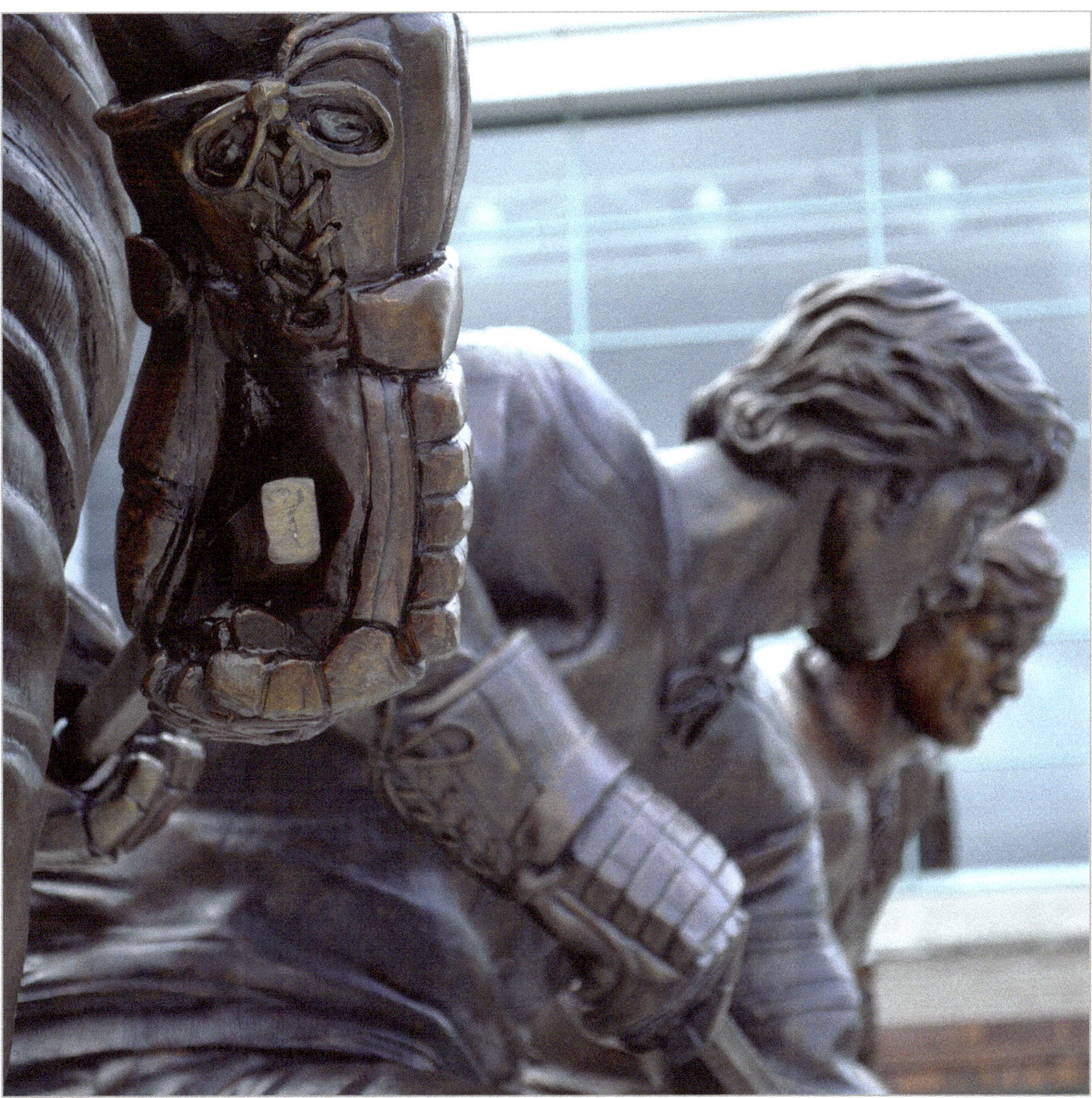

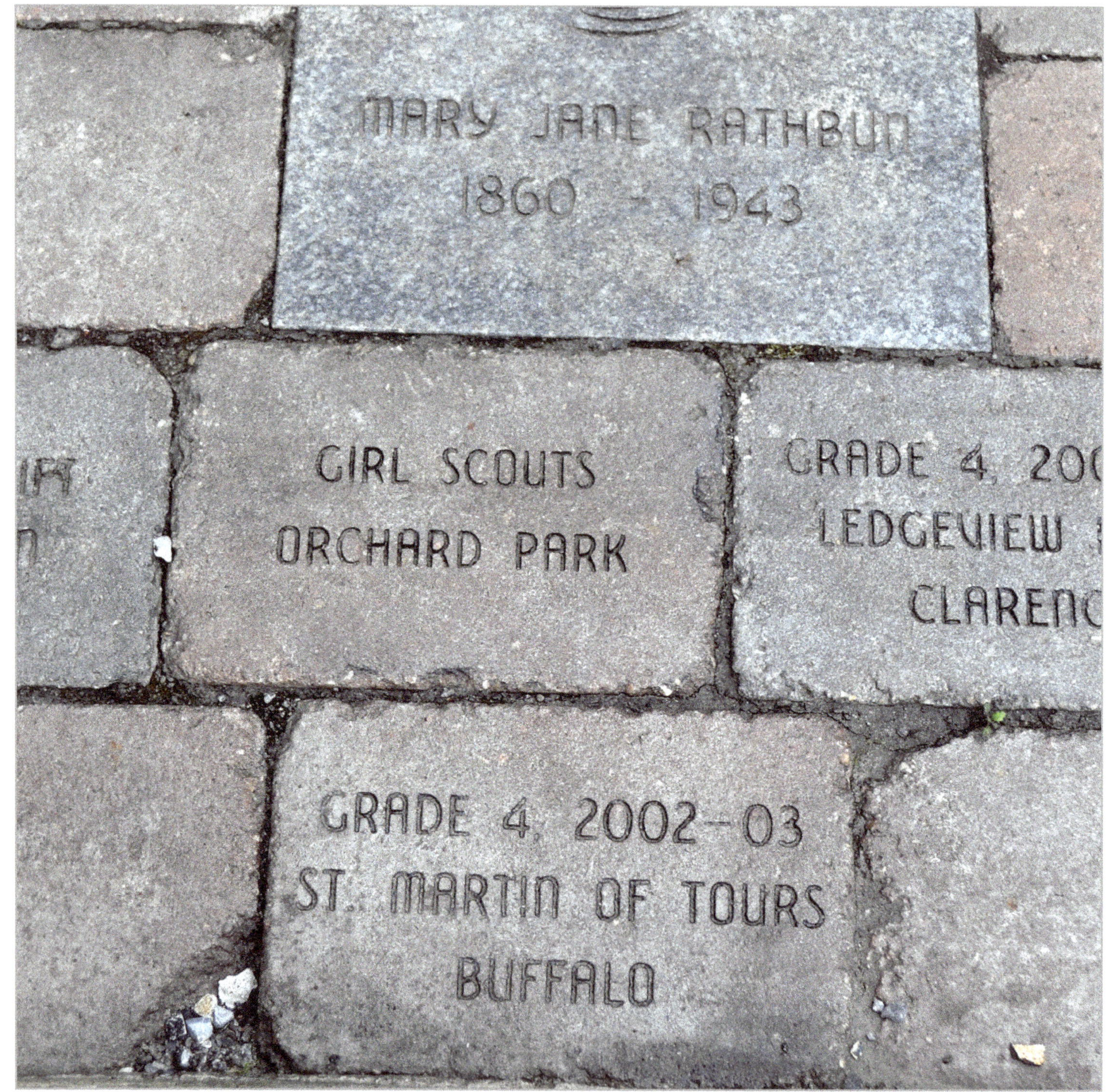
MARY JANE RATHBUN
1860 - 1943
GIRL SCOUTS
ORCHARD PARK
GRADE 4, 200
LEDGEVIEW
CLAREN
GRADE 4, 2002-03
ST. MARTIN OF TOURS
BUFFALO

# Standing on the shoulders of giants

It's cheaper than skywriting, and far less messy than hiding a ring in your girlfriend's mashed potatoes. Ask: "Will you marry me?" with a brick.

Bricks for Buffalo is a civic project initiated in 2001 consisting of two paths: the Plaza Walkway and the Women's Walkway. They cover more than 8,000 square feet on the waterfront behind First Niagara Center and contain more than 700 personalized cobblestone bricks, granite stones and benches.

The Women's Walkway was a joint project of the Women's Pavilion Pan-Am 2001 and Working For Downtown to celebrate the 100-year anniversary of the Pan-American Exposition. One hundred women, now deceased, were chosen for their profound contributions to Western New York, and each is honored with a commemorative granite stone and description in the Women's Walkway brochure.

The Women's Walkway also contains cobblestone bricks and granite benches which were purchased to honor the women in our lives.

40

**Bricks for Buffalo /Women's Walkway**
Foot of Main Street, behind First Niagara Center, Buffalo, NY 14203

# Where the buffalo roam

Bison. Sure, we have them at the zoo. One was even spotted on a grassy median in downtown Buffalo. Despite being a half a world away, they also roam in Dortmund, Germany and in Kanazawa, Japan. The explanation is easy. They were birthday gifts from their sister, Buffalo.

Sculptor Cecilia Evans Taylor, best known for her bronze sculptures of animals, created a football-sized bison as a bicentennial project for Church Street Park in downtown Buffalo. Identical bison sculptures were presented to Buffalo's sister cities of Kanazawa, Japan in 1966 and Dortmund, Germany in 1982.

In the 1960s, a group of citizens established a cultural exchange between the city of Buffalo and Kanazawa, Japan. Now, more than fifty years later, it's one of the oldest cultural exchanges in the country. The Buffalo-Kanazawa sister city connection has produced a long list of accomplishments that includes the creation of the beautiful Japanese Garden on the grounds of the Buffalo History Museum along Mirror Lake. Completed in 1974, the Buffalo Japanese Garden was donated by the people of Kanazawa, Japan. In honor of the 50th Anniversary of this collaboration, Japan also donated twenty cherry blossom trees.

Buffalo is proud to now have sixteen Sister Cities. These links with other cities around the world have increased our awareness of other cultures.

**"Bison," by Cecilia Evans Taylor**
Main and North Division Streets, Buffalo, NY 14202

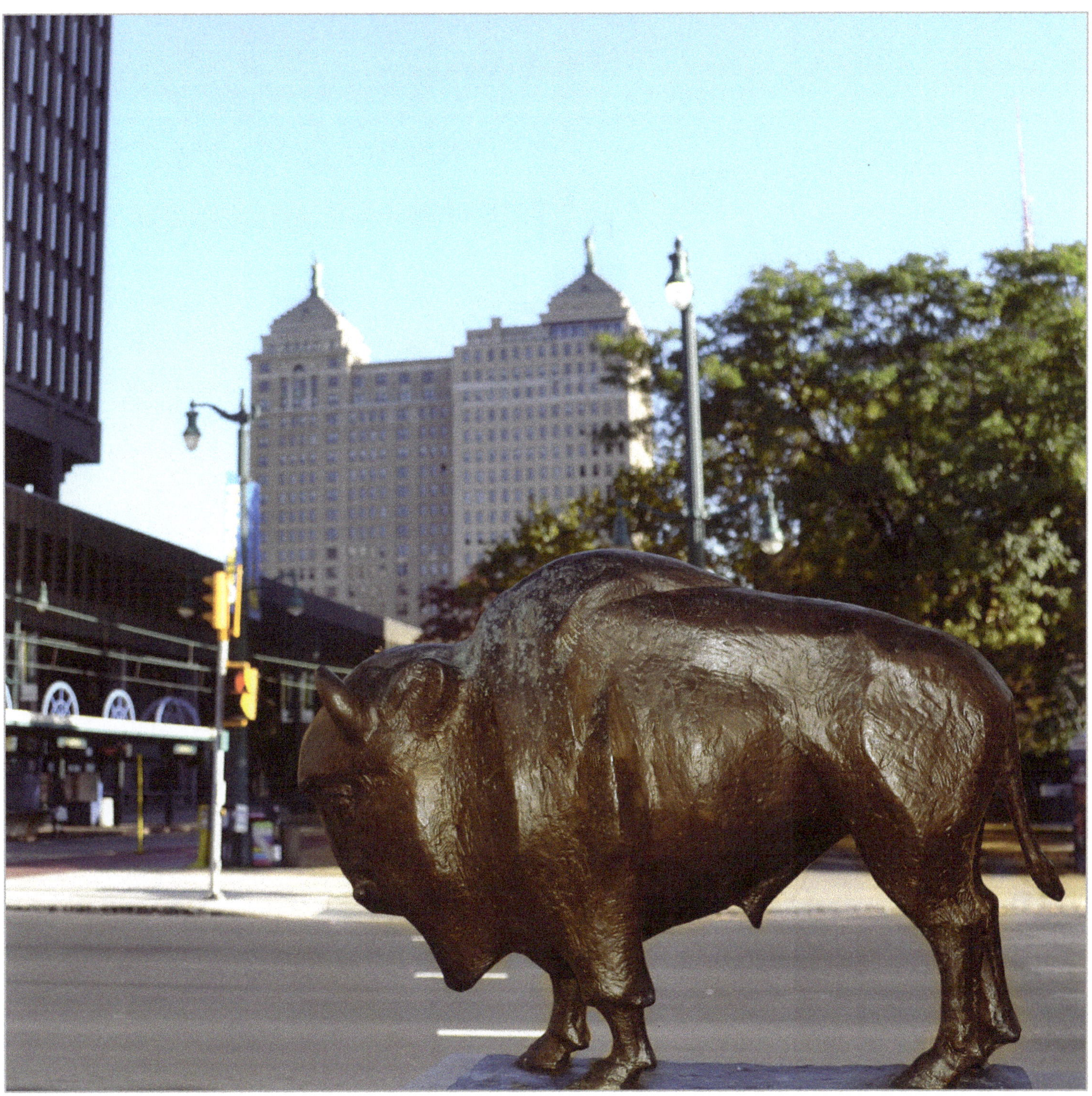

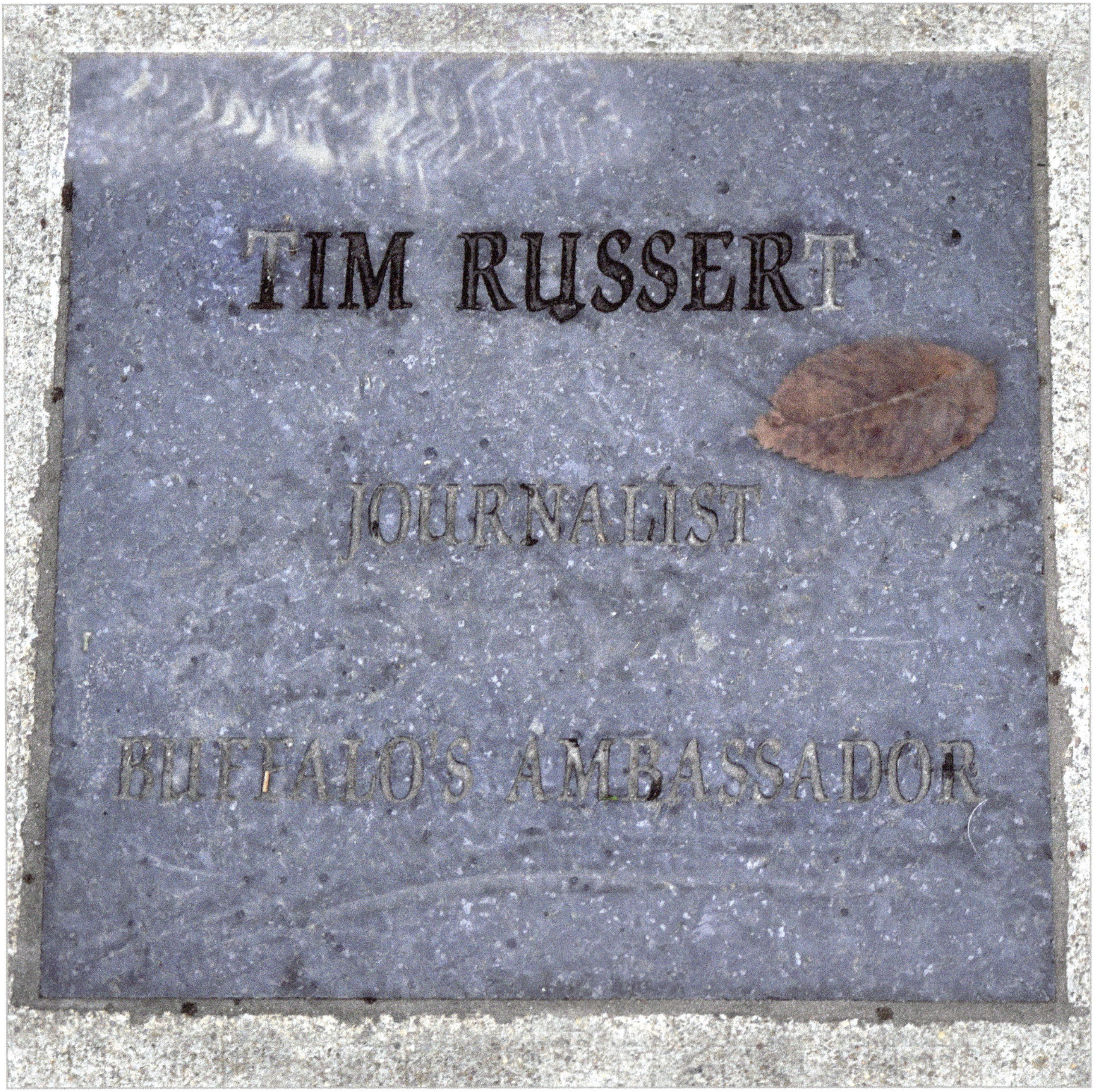

TIM RUSSERT

JOURNALIST

BUFFALO'S AMBASSADOR

# Go Bills!

The next time you walk across Bidwell Parkway at Elmwood, look down and be inspired. You are standing among Buffalo's best and brightest.

The Buffalo Cultural Walk of Fame, a project driven by the passion and dedication of Charles Griffasi Sr., was created to honor the many Western New Yorkers who have enriched the world with their artistic contributions. To celebrate the legacy of our vast heritage, their names are engraved in granite plaques and permanently recessed into the sidewalk.

A recent inductee was hands down Buffalo's greatest cheerleader not wearing spandex. Tim Russert is an amazing success story. From growing up in a working-class neighborhood of South Buffalo, Russert rose to the coveted job of Washington Bureau Chief of NBC News and moderator of Meet the Press. He proved that nice guys don't always finish last. Unfortunately he also proved another adage – the good die young.

As an honoree, Russert has some very prominent company. He joins Western New York notables such as Lucille Ball, Tom Fontana, Leonard Pennario, Amanda Blake, Rick James, Charles Burchfield, Harold Arlen, Grover Washington Sr., Mark Twain, and many others.

The Cultural Walk of Fame is worth a stroll.

**42**

**The Buffalo Cultural Walk of Fame**
Elmwood Avenue at Bidwell, Buffalo, NY 14222

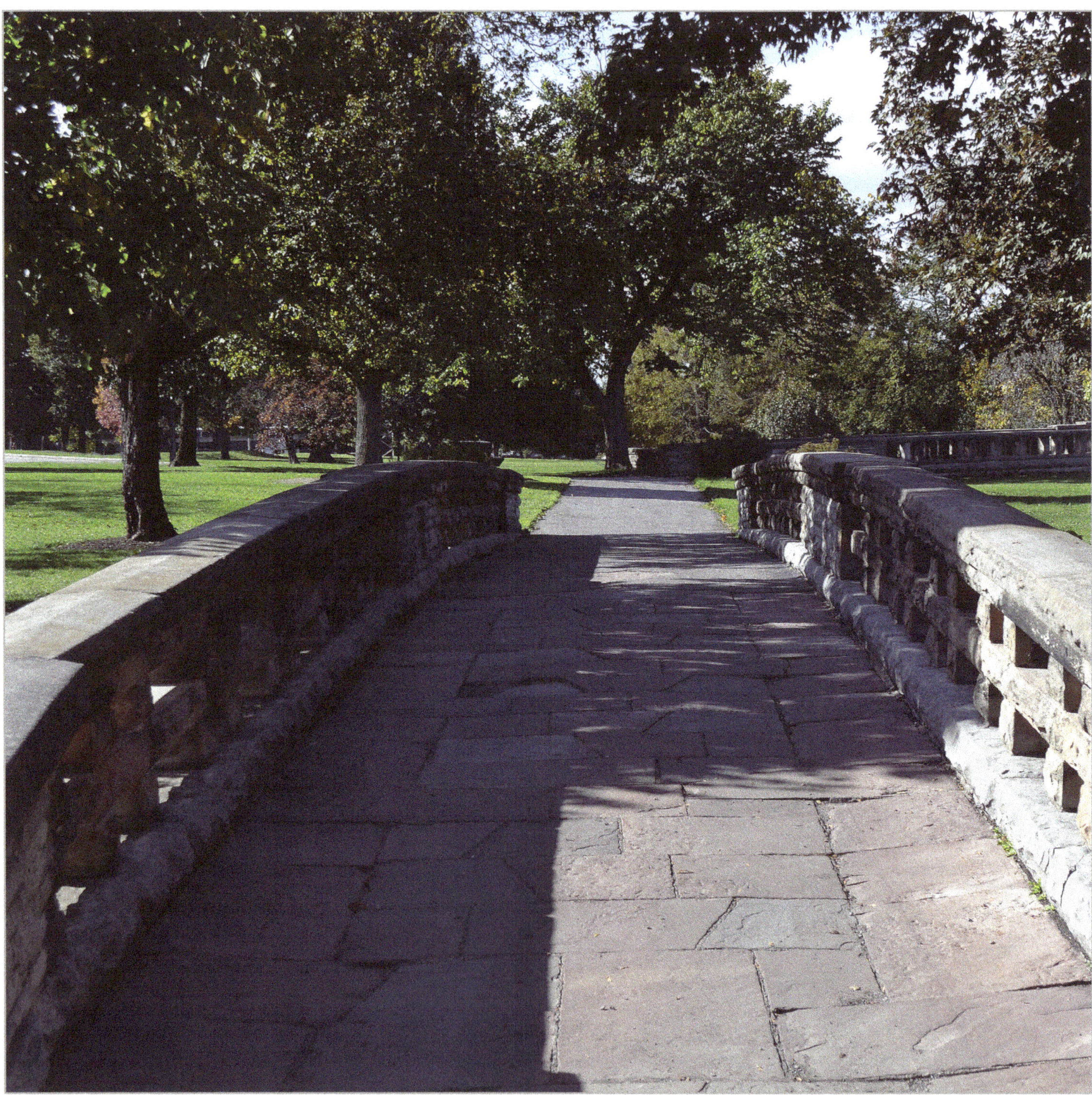

# The way to the secret garden

In Delaware Park, just west of the Parkside Lodge, is a curious stone walkway that seemingly connects nothing to nothing. If you peer over the side of the stone walls you will see a rolling lawn. You'll also be looking at Buffalo's dirtiest secret. More accurately, it's Buffalo's biggest secret covered with dirt.

You see, this isn't really a walkway. It's what remains of a stone arch bridge, much like the one that crosses Hoyt Lake on the other side of the park. Beneath it is the historic Delaware Park Quarry Garden, now covered with soil from the excavated Scajaquada Expressway. The view from the bridge must have been magnificent as it overlooked three large reflecting pools named Floral, Shady and Long, all interconnected by a series of scenic bridges and walkways.

In the early 1800s, before the creation of Delaware Park, this spot was a working Onondaga limestone quarry that provided cut stone for the city. As part of Frederick Law Olmsted and Calvert Vaux's vision of Delaware Park, this former quarry, nicknamed "the ledges," was morphed into a stunning garden. It included a series of connecting ponds and bridal paths and landscaping that seamlessly blended with its stone cliff background.

In 1912, the bowling (bocce) greens were constructed along Parkside Avenue, and an 18-hole golf course was carved out of the portion of the park known as "the Meadows." Parkside Lodge was built in 1914 to serve as a locker room for both.

Construction of the Scajaquada and Kensington Expressways began in the early 1960s, radically cutting up a large portion of the Olmsted Parkway System and carving a giant trench through the heart of the city. Many of the tons of rock and landfill were disposed of by filling in the Quarry Garden.

On a brighter note, the Buffalo Olmsted Parks Conservancy, as part of its new master plan, is committed to uncovering this wonderous secret garden. Stay tuned!

**43**

**Delaware Park - near Parkside Lodge**
104 Parkside Avenue, Buffalo, NY 14214

# From working stiff to working stiff

They stream down what seems to be an endlessly descending escalator by the thousands. Carrying briefcases, lunchboxes, and massive backpacks, they flood the Humboldt/Hospital subway station each morning preparing to get to wherever they need to go to grind out another day. As they reach the space between the inbound and outbound platform they suddenly come face-to-face with people who have just finished a hard shift.

They've just met some of Milton Rogovin's "Forgotten Ones."

Milton Rogovin was a world famous social documentarian whose life's work became photographing people who were invisible to others. Blacklisted in the Red scare of the 1950s, Rogovin was forced to close his Buffalo optometry practice and chose to dedicate his life to raising our awareness of social and economic inequities through photography. His brutally frank and unassuming pictures captured the lives of the working class poor and dispossessed.

Armed with nothing more than a vintage Rolleiflex, a roll of film, and his dedicated wife Anne who was always there to blaze a trail in front of him, they traveled to Appalachia, Chile and Mexico to take portraits of working people. His subjects were ordinary people in poor neighborhoods, from the Lower West Side of Buffalo and Black churches, to Native Americans on reservations. Coal miners and steel workers had an advocate in Milton, allowing him to take their pictures at work as well as inviting him into their homes.

Some of Milton Rogivin's most brilliant work occured when many years later he rephotographed some of his original subjects and displayed them as a series.

**Milton Rogovin "Forgotten Ones" Photographs**
Humboldt/Hospital Metrorail Station
2085 Main Street at Kensington, Buffalo, NY 14214

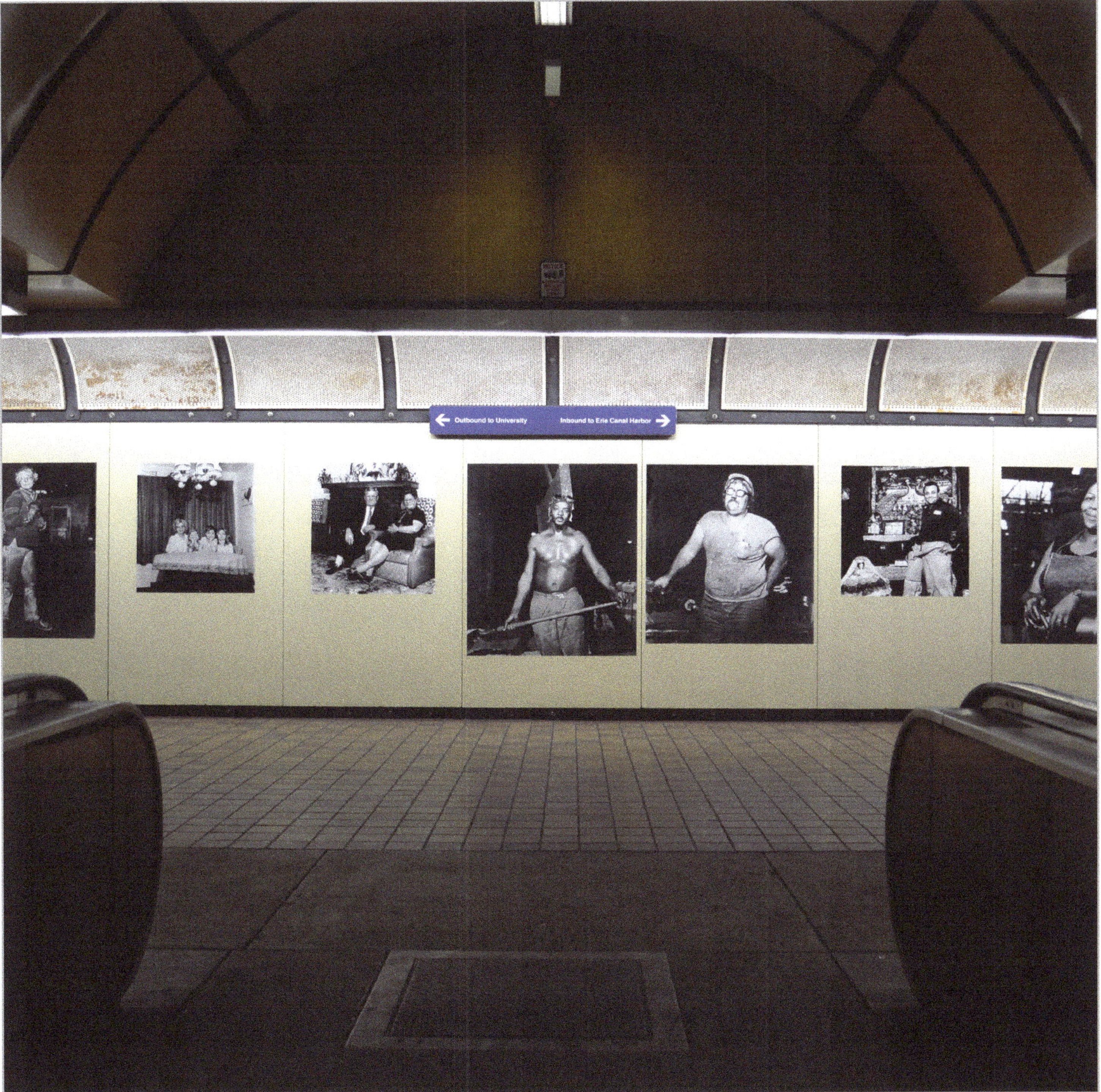
← Outbound to University
Inbound to Erie Canal Harbor →

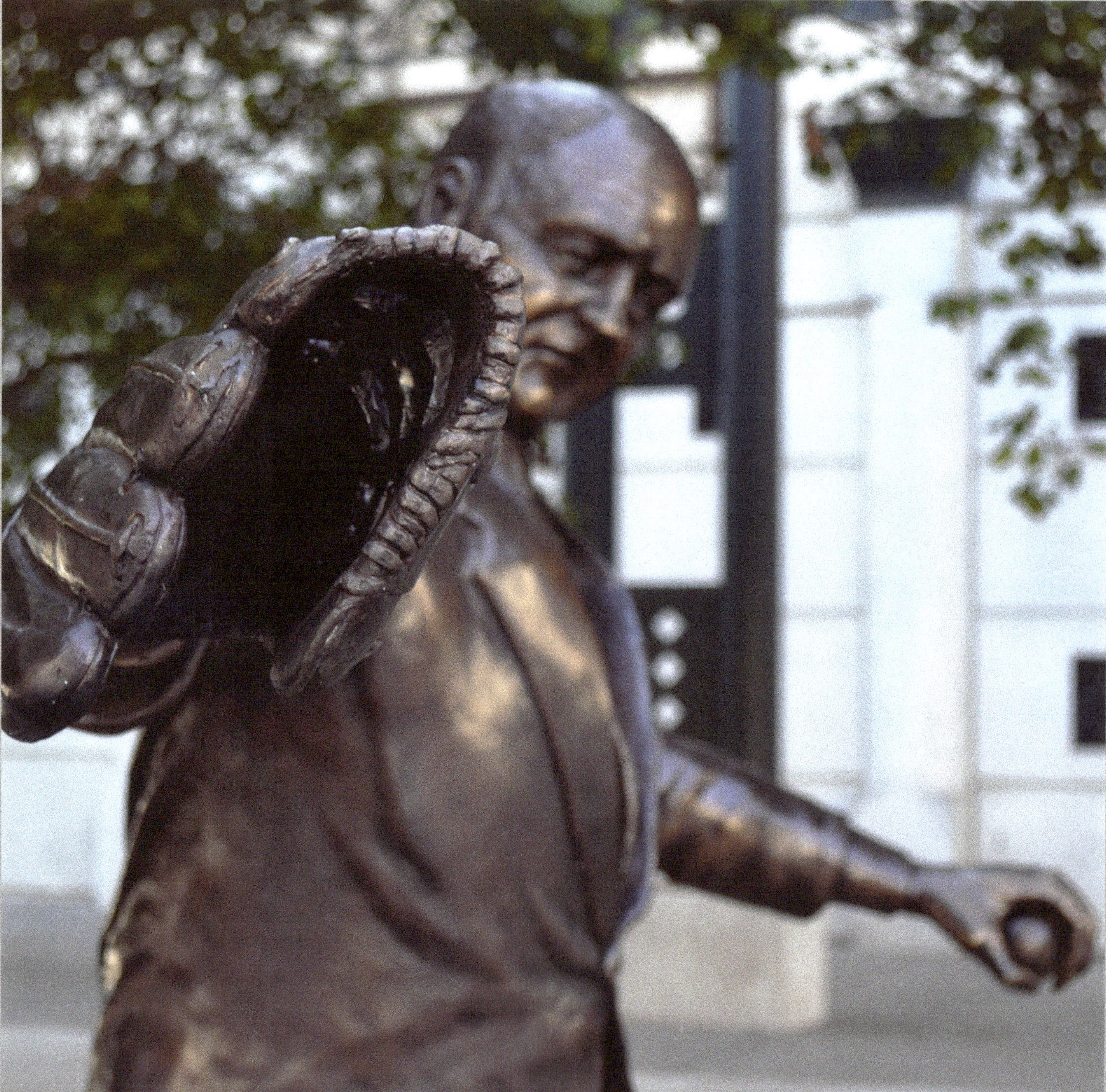

# Build it and they will come

All this story lacks is a cornfield.

Ever since 1879 there has been a baseball team wearing a Buffalo Bisons uniform. In 1983 Rich Products expanded beyond food products with the purchase of the Buffalo Bisons minor league baseball team. When new owners Bob and Mindy Rich first considered the idea of bringing big-league baseball to Buffalo, they knew that a big-league stadium would be a prerequisite. Build it and they will come.

Jimmy Griffin, Buffalo's longest serving mayor and a lifelong baseball fan, must have also heard the voice and fully jumped on board with the dream. Hizzoner was relentless in increasing the presence of baseball in the city of Buffalo, going to great lengths to support the city's push for a major league team – as well as in the development of a stadium right in the heart of downtown.

In 1988, a retro-designed baseball stadium, originally named Pilot Field, made its triumphant debut. Buffalo was now at the vanguard of teaching the country how to integrate a new light-rail-accessible, downtown stadium with a daytime workforce and existing parking infrastructure.

While the original goal of bringing a major league team to Buffalo has yet to be achieved, this is still a remarkable success story. Fans showed up in numbers never before seen in minor league history, often drawing more than a million people each season.

Jimmy Griffin, a season ticket holder and infamous shagger of foul balls, proved himself in both word and deed as one of the Bison's most passionate fans. In August 2012, a life-sized statue was dedicated to him just outside the stadium gates. It was created by local artist William Koch based on a photograph of Griffin throwing a pitch at the ballpark.

45

**"Jimmy Griffin," by William Koch**
Coca-Cola Field
275 Washington St, Buffalo, NY 14203

# Geriatric arboriculture

If you're a tree hugger, you're going to need really long arms to get around this senior citizen.

On Franklin Street, between Edward and Virginia streets, sits a massive hulk among the sycamore trees. In 1960, the Buffalo Lumber Exchange bolted a plaque on it proclaiming it to be the oldest tree in the city, estimated to be as much as 250 years old. That would now make it over 300 years old. Most amazing is that it sprouted up precisely between where the city eventually constructed the sidewalk and the street. What luck.

However, before we coronate this sycamore tree as officially "Buffalo's oldest," the fans of the spectacular Great Oak located in the middle of the Delaware Park Golf Course say not so fast.

According to an April 9, 2007, Buffalo News article, "Olmsted Parks Conservancy tree care supervisior Jeff Brett, a certified arborist, thinks that's not only the oldest oak in the city but the oldest tree - it's slower growing and, because it's in the open, wouldn't reach the same height as the sycamore, although getting much wider. The problem with trees this size is that they're too big for a complete core drilling, so the only way to count the annual growth rings is to cut the tree down - which seems a tad drastic, not to mention self-defeating."

I guess the only way left to settle the matter is to count the candles on their birthday cakes.

As a sidenote, in front of Keller Brothers & Miller print shop, directly across the street from the 300-year-old tree is a wood carving of Ben Franklin. It was created by Rick Pratt from a 100-year-old Silver Maple tree damaged in the October 2006 Storm.

**46**

**Oldest Tree In Buffalo Plaque**
Franklin Street between Edward and Virginia, Buffalo, NY 14202

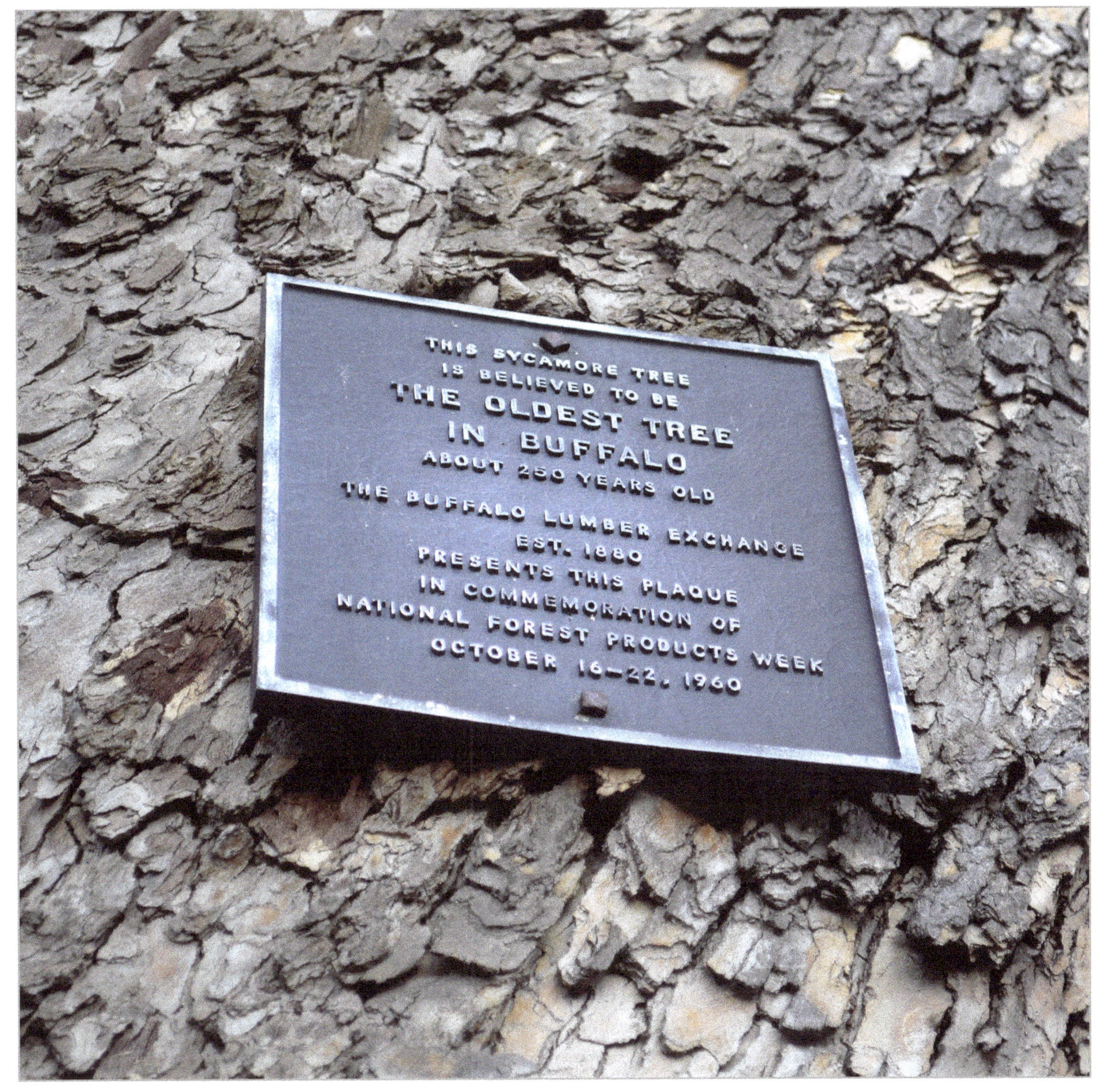
THIS SYCAMORE TREE
IS BELIEVED TO BE
THE OLDEST TREE
IN BUFFALO
ABOUT 250 YEARS OLD
THE BUFFALO LUMBER EXCHANGE
EST. 1880
PRESENTS THIS PLAQUE
IN COMMEMORATION OF
NATIONAL FOREST PRODUCTS WEEK
OCTOBER 16-22, 1960

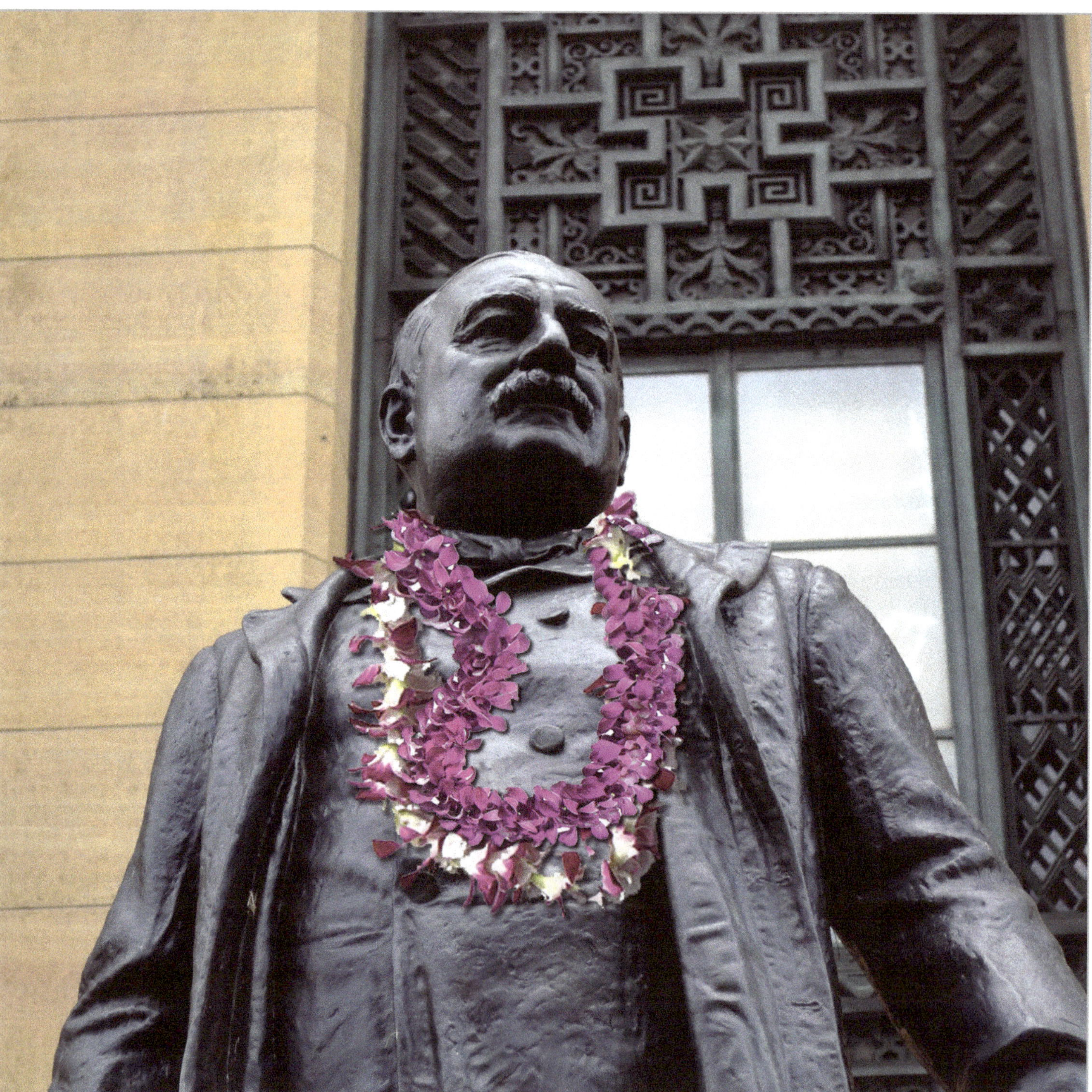

# Aloha, Grover

Bryant Baker, a British-born American artist, is famous for sculpting five U.S. presidents, three of which are at Buffalo City Hall.

Adorning the corners of the building are two fifteen-feet statues that were unveiled together during the dedication of the new City Hall in 1936.

On the northeast corner of the building facing Niagara Square is Millard Fillmore, the thirteenth President. He is represented standing in a rather arrogant pose, hip thrust out, nose in the air, and wearing a cape. Baker did a masterful job disguising his monumentally bad comb-over.

On the southeast corner is Grover Cleveland, mayor of Buffalo, sheriff of Erie County, governor of New York, and President twice, from 1885 to 1889 and 1893 to 1897. He can be seen wearing an overcoat, double breasted jacket, bow tie, and occasionally colorful Hawaiian leis. No, the statue doesn't take vacations in Hawaii, Hawaiians travel to Buffalo to honor Cleveland. He is revered for championing Hawaiian rights and national sovereignty in the 1890s, even as sugar plantation owners were overthrowing Hawaiian Queen Liliuokalani and seeking annexation to the United States.

The bronze bust of John F. Kennedy that sits atop a polished pink marble base in the City Hall lobby was also sculpted by Baker twenty-eight years later.

47

**"Grover Cleveland," by Bryant Baker**
Buffalo City Hall
65 Niagara Square, Buffalo, NY 14202

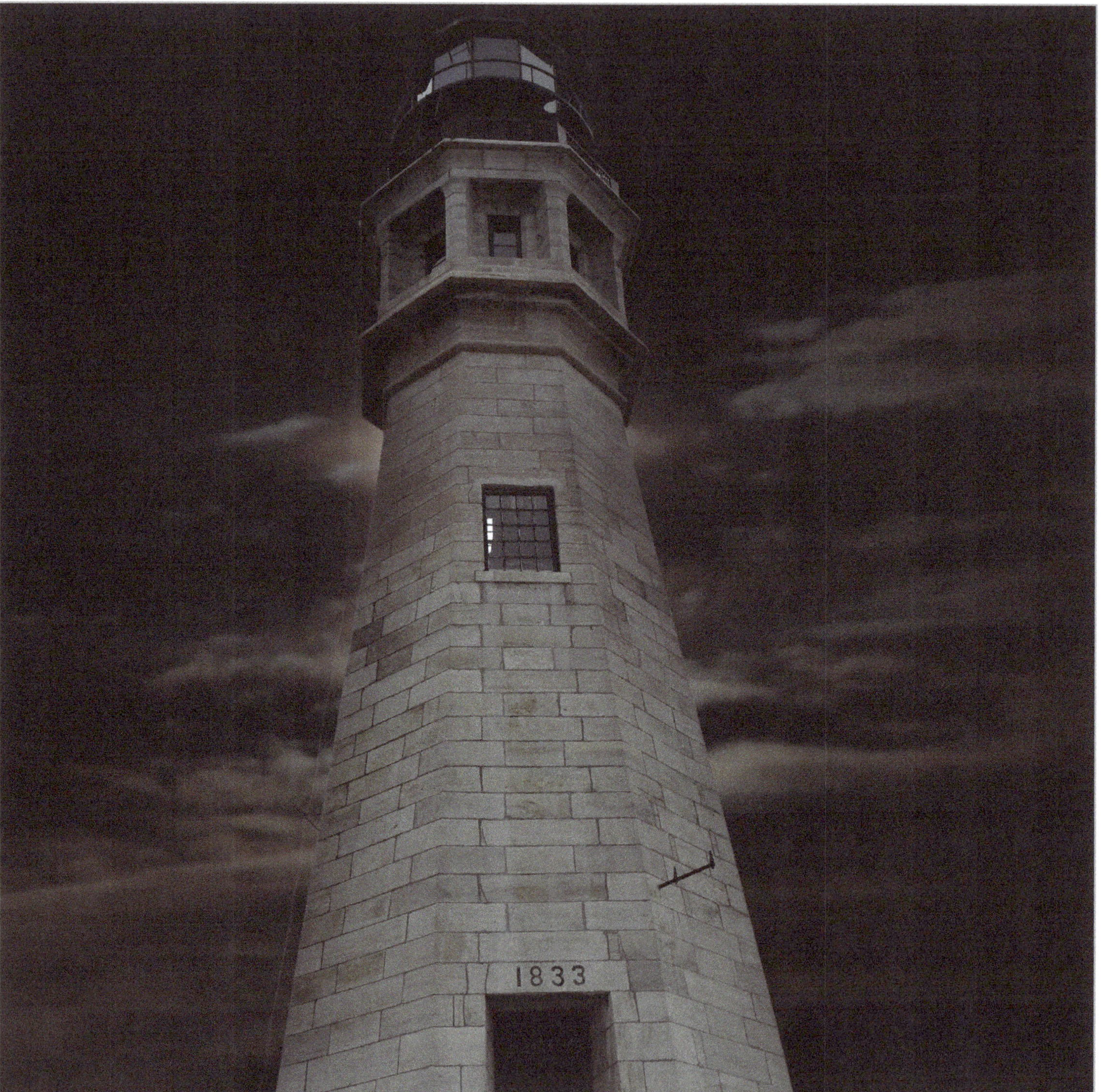

# Still beaming

Built in 1833, the Buffalo Lighthouse is one of our city's most enduring symbols. When you pass by it leaving the inner harbor on the Spirit of Buffalo, or are simply enjoying its beauty from the Hatch across the river, you're not just looking at the oldest standing building in Buffalo, you're also surveying one of the oldest lighthouses on the Great Lakes. It's even on the city's official seal.

When the Erie Canal opened in 1825 a new lighthouse was needed to direct one of the busiest ports in the world. During the meteoric growth of the nineteenth century, this forty-four-feet octagonal limestone tower served the city well. It was formally deactivated in 1914 and replaced by an outer harbor breakwater light that was more visible to lake traffic.

The Buffalo Lighthouse is often called the Chinaman's Light. That's the nickname first given to a wooden structure used as a lookout point built on a pier 150-feet west of the lighthouse. It's said that the roof resembled a Chinese coolie's hat. When this structure was torn down, the moniker somehow stuck to the Buffalo Lighthouse.

In the mid-1950s, absorbed as part of the Coast Guard base and facing demolition by neglect, our iconic beacon of light arguably launched Buffalo's present day preservation movement. In 1958, the Army Corps of Engineers planned to demolish the Lighthouse as part of a river-widening project, which triggered a loud public outcry.

The lighthouse was saved in 1961 by the hard work of a group of community-minded citizens and the Buffalo and Erie County Historical Society. The Buffalo Lighthouse Association, formed in 1985, now leases the structure from the Coast Guard and is responsible for restoration and site development work. A pedestrian walkway along the south bank of the Buffalo River now allows public access to the grounds during daylight hours. Bathed in spotlights and using a special low light to avoid confusing boaters, the lighthouse is now beautifully aglow at night.

**48**

**Buffalo Lighthouse**
U.S. Coast Guard Base at the mouth of the Buffalo River

# Art is hope

In the main atrium of the Roswell Park Cancer Institute, brightly illuminated by a wall of windows overlooking a spacious garden, sits a boisterously colorful sculpture. This seventeen-feet metal work was to be my final shot for this book. Since sculptures rarely wiggle, need to stop and comb their hair, or blink at inappropriate times, this was supposed to be an uneventful photo shoot. A quick ten clicks or so, positioned at various angles and I'd be in, out, and done.

I was just about to wrap up and rush back to work when out of seemingly nowhere came a soft voice.

"Will you take my picture before I die?"

I looked up and there stood a small, middle-aged woman, obviously bald under her hastily tied bandana, holding out her hand for me to shake.

She respectfully repeated her question, "Will you take my picture before I die?"

Her name was Denise, no last name volunteered. Ravaged by breast cancer, she had arrived at Roswell Park early that day only to receive the most devastating of news.

Feeling dwarfed by her courage, I had her pose next to the sculpture. Denise and her brave yet serene smile will now live forever in my book. Promise kept.

Aptly entitled "Hope," this sculpture was created by Buffalo artist Ellen Steinfeld.

49

**"Hope," by Ellen Steinfeld**
Roswell Park Cancer Institute - Main Lobby
Elm and Carlton streets, Buffalo, NY 14263

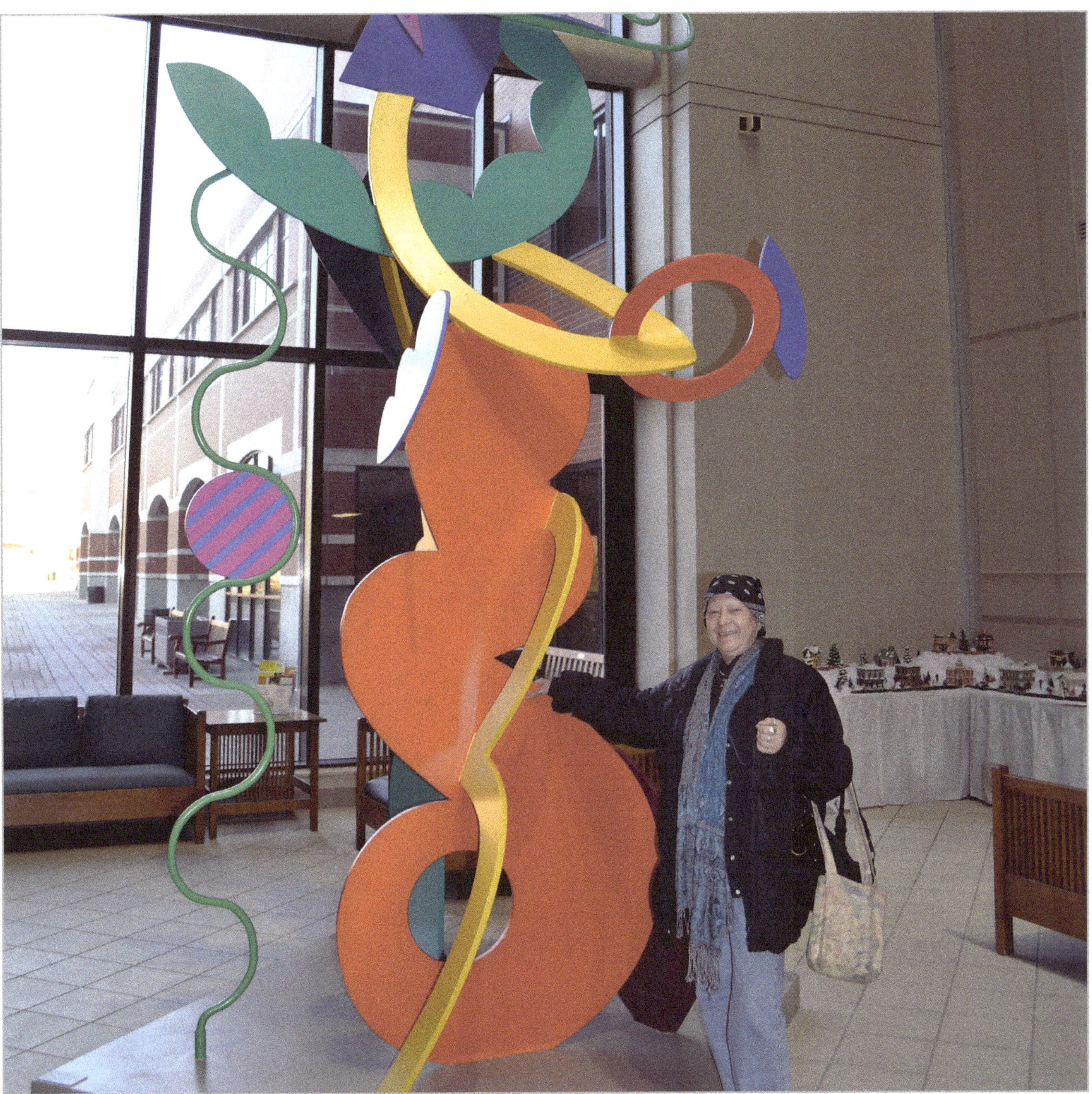

# A very special thanks:

I've learned that while it may take a village to raise a child, it takes an entire city to write a book. While I'd like to sincerely thank everyone in the phonebook, I've taken my trusty yellow marker and highlighted a few of those who have gone well beyond the call of duty. Their passion for this city has helped create a vast ocean of resources and institutional knowledge without which creating this book would have been utterly impossible.

Chuck LaChiusa who selflessly created and maintains the totally amazing "Buffalo as an Architectural Museum" website, Buffaloah.com.

Western New York Heritage Press and their must-read quarterly magazine.

The Buffalo Arts Commission public arts online website for providing a solid starting point for exploration.

Martha Neri and Jim Mendola, archivists at the Buffalo Olmsted Parks Conservancy, for flushing-out the research equivilant of a needle in a haystack.

Dan Sack for his photo and timely resources on the "Buffalo Blue Light District."

Paula Devereaux's giant chicken "Red" for posing so nicely on short notice.

Dylan Heyworth for his ability to imagine the Richardson Olmsted Complex through the eyes of a six-year-old.

Marti Gorman for her uncanny ability to use the Rosetta Stone to translate my guttural ramblings into readable English.

And of course, my wife Laura and wonderful family for putting up with my malarkey.

### The King of B.S.

For an all-girls school, this is a very unusual way to decorate the main entrance.

50

**Buffalo Seminary**
205 Bidwell Parkway, Buffalo, NY 14222

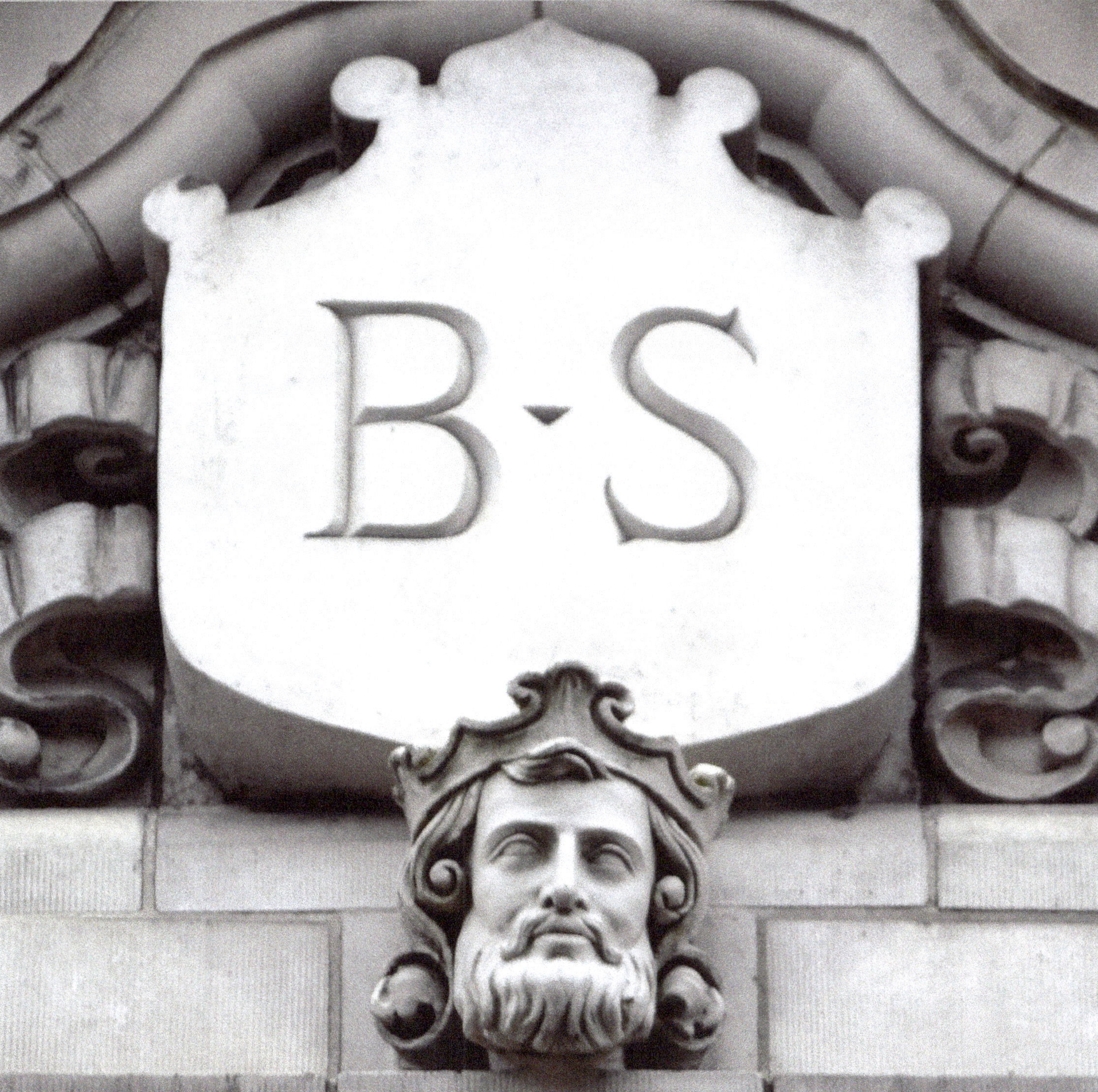

# Index



## The classics in drivetime

The statue of Wolfgang Amadeus Mozart car-watching along the Scajaquada expressway is a constant reminder to change the radio to an NPR station. The statue's base lists his greatest hits: "Le Nozze di Figaro," "Il Don Giovanni," "Die Zauberflöete," and "Requiem."



**"Wolfgang A. Mozart," by Olin H. Warner**
Delaware Park near Scajaquada Expressway, Buffalo, NY 14216

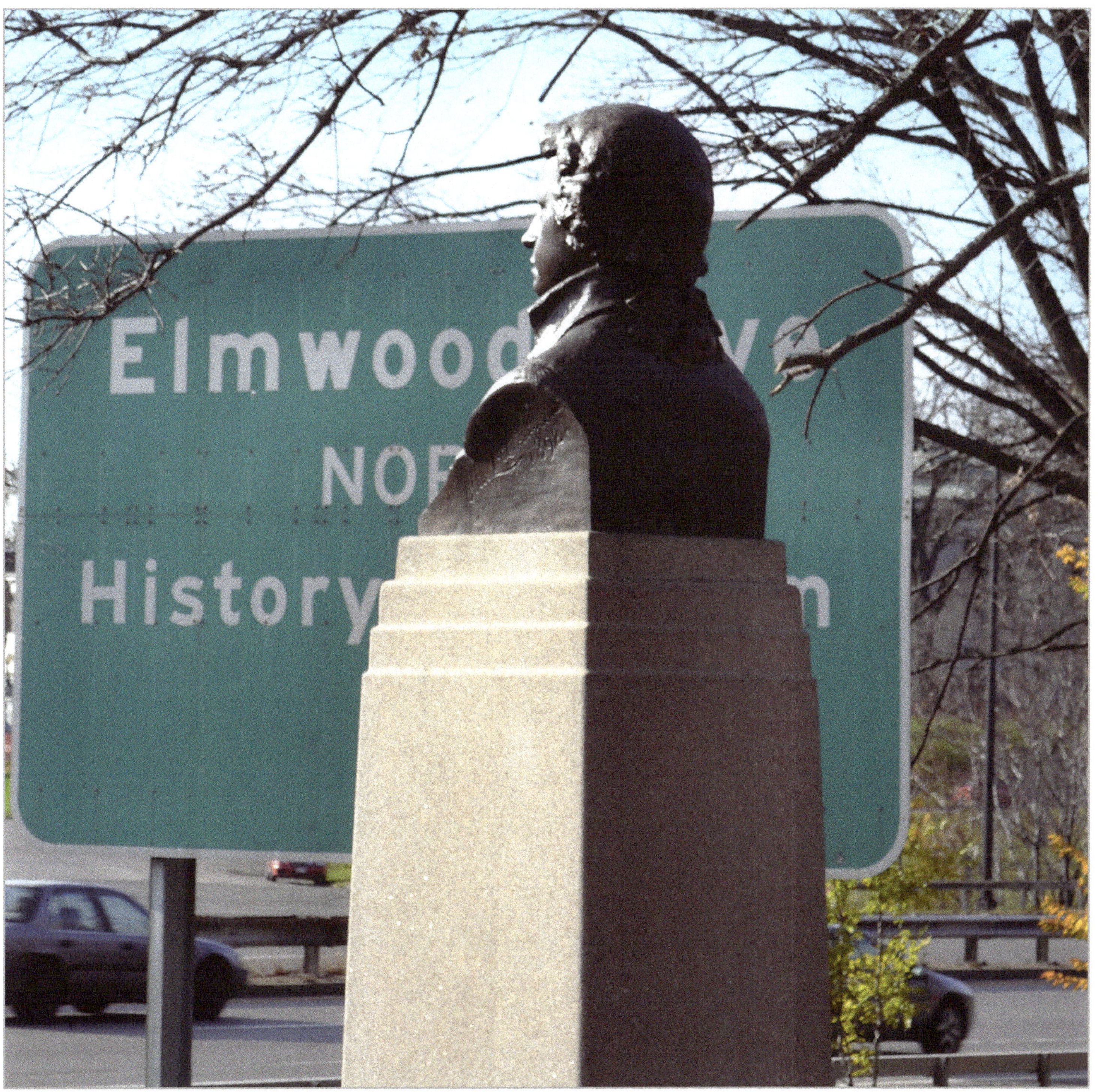
Elmwood
NOR
History

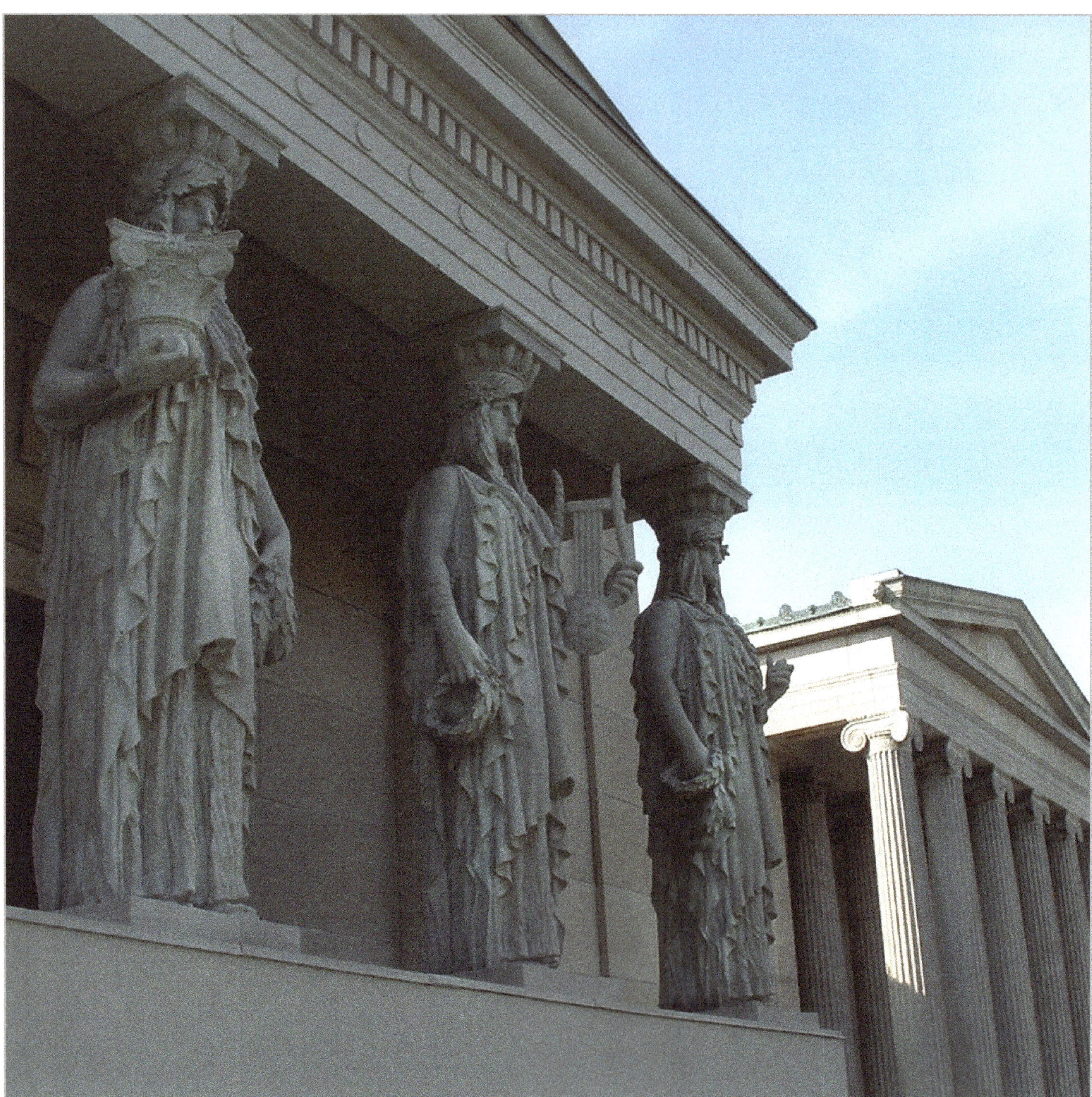

## The Supremes

The caryatids representing the Music muse and her back-up band were four years late for their first gig. The Albright-Knox Art Gallery was originally intended to be used as the Fine Arts Pavilion for the Pan-American Exposition in 1901. However, construction delays postponed completion until 1905, well after the Pan-Am was torn down.

**Caryatids, by Augustus Saint-Gaudens**
Albright-Knox Art Gallery, South Portico - 1285 Elmwood Avenue, Buffalo, NY 14222

# ■ Map Index

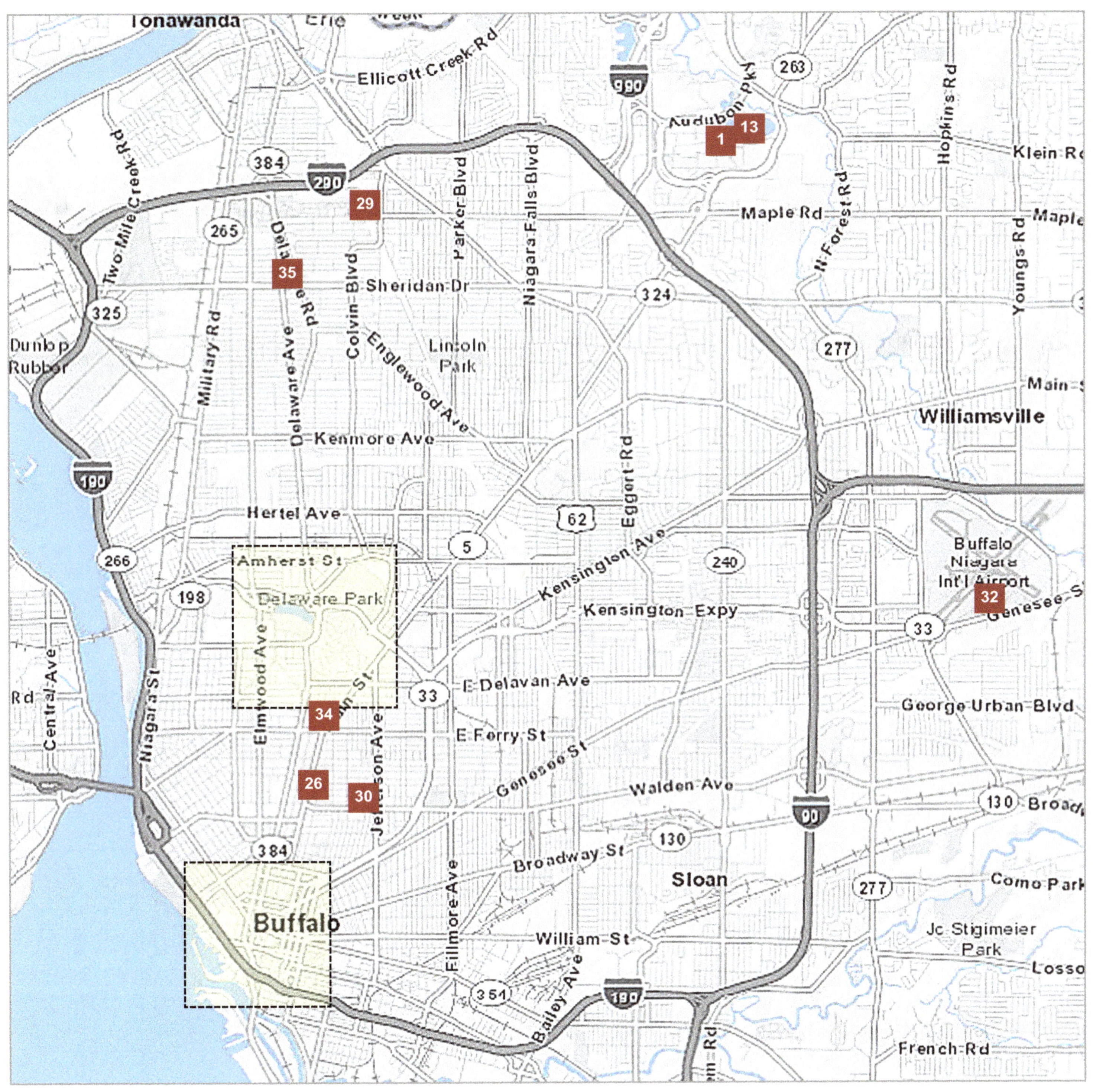

Tonawanda
Erie
Ellicott Creek Rd
990
263
Audubon Pky
1
13
Hopkins Rd
Klein Rd
384
290
Maple Rd
Maple
29
265
Parker Blvd
Niagara Falls Blvd
324
N Forest Rd
Youngs Rd
Delaware Ave Rd
35
Sheridan Dr
Colvin Blvd
277
325
Englewood Ave
Lincoln Park
Main St
Dunlop Rubber
Military Rd
Kenmore Ave
Williamsville
Hertel Ave
62
Buffalo Niagara Int'l Airport
266
Amherst St
5
Kensington Ave
240
32
Genesee St
198
Delaware Park
Kensington Expy
33
Central Ave
Elmwood Ave
St
E Delavan Ave
George Urban Blvd
Niagara St
34
33
E Ferry St
26
Genesee St
Walden Ave
30
Jefferson Ave
Broadway St
130
Broad
384
Como Park
Sloan
277
Buffalo
Jc Stigmeier Park
Fillmore Ave
William St
130
Losso
190
351
Bailey Ave
190
Rd
French Rd

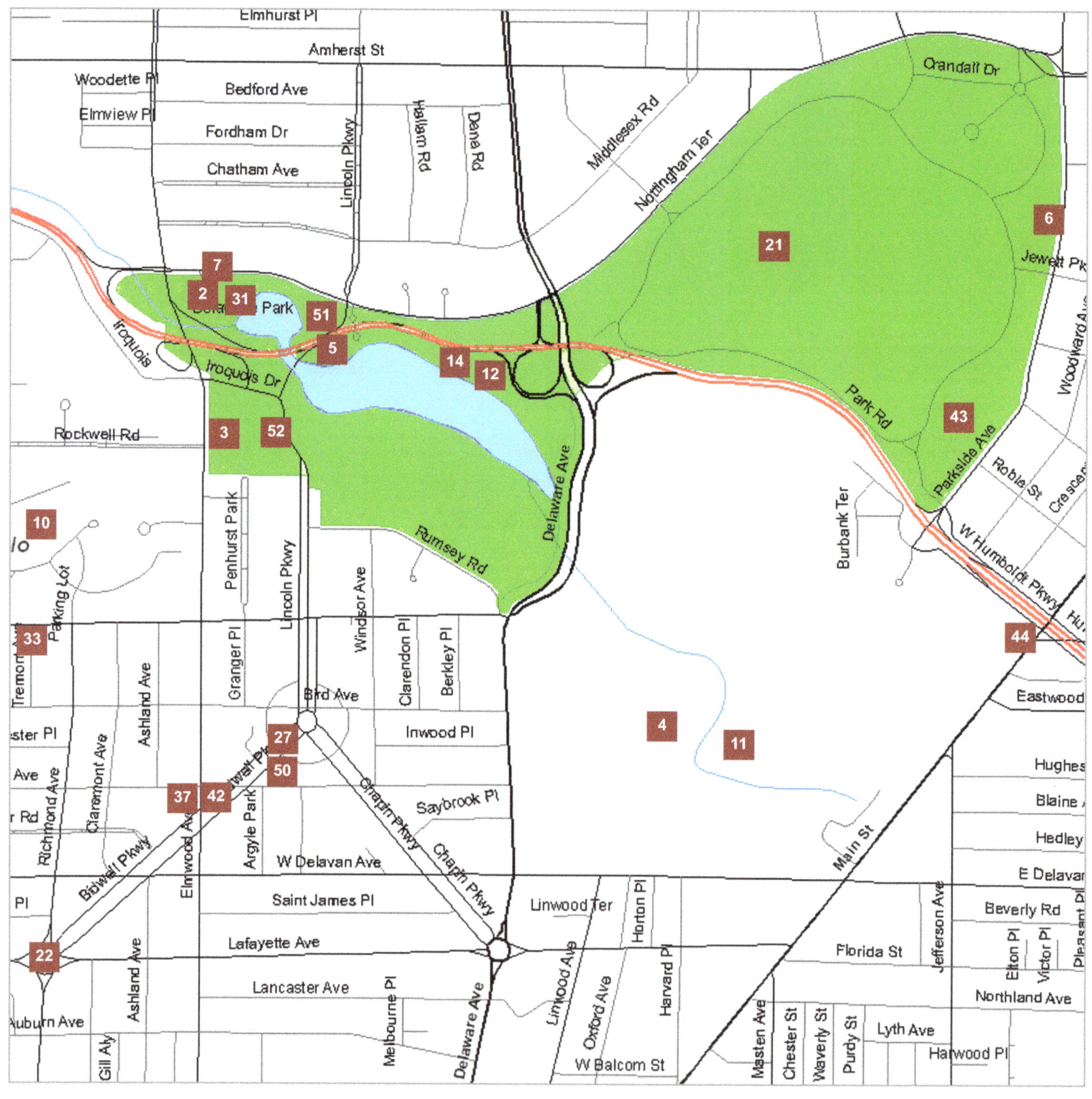

Elmhurst Pl
Amherst St
Crandall Dr
Woodette Pl
Bedford Ave
Elmview Pl
Fordham Dr
Chatham Ave
Middlesex Rd
Nottingham Ter
Lincoln Pkwy
Hallam Rd
Dana Rd
6
21
Jewett Pky
7
Woodward Ave
2
31
Delaware Park
51
5
Iroquois
14
12
Iroquois Dr
Park Rd
43
Parkside Ave
3
52
Roble St
Crescent
Delaware Ave
Rockwell Rd
Rumsey Rd
10
Penhurst Park
Burbank Ter
W Humboldt Pkwy
Parking Lot
Lincoln Pkwy
Windsor Ave
33
44
Tremont
Ashland Ave
Granger Pl
Clarendon Pl
Berkley Pl
Eastwood
Bird Ave
Hughes
4
11
Inwood Pl
27
Claremont Ave
Blaine
50
Hedley
37
42
Argyle Park
Elmwood Ave
Bidwell Pky
Chapin Pkwy
Saybrook Pl
Main St
E Delavan
Richmond Ave
W Delavan Ave
Chapin Pkwy
Jefferson Ave
Beverly Rd
22
Saint James Pl
Linwood Ter
Horton Pl
Harvard Pl
Elton Pl
Victor Pl
Pleasant
Lafayette Ave
Linwood Ave
Oxford Ave
Florida St
Ashland Ave
Masten Ave
Northland Ave
Lancaster Ave
Melbourne Pl
Chester St
Waverly St
Purdy St
Lyth Ave
Auburn Ave
Gill Aly
Delaware Ave
W Balcom St
Harwood Pl

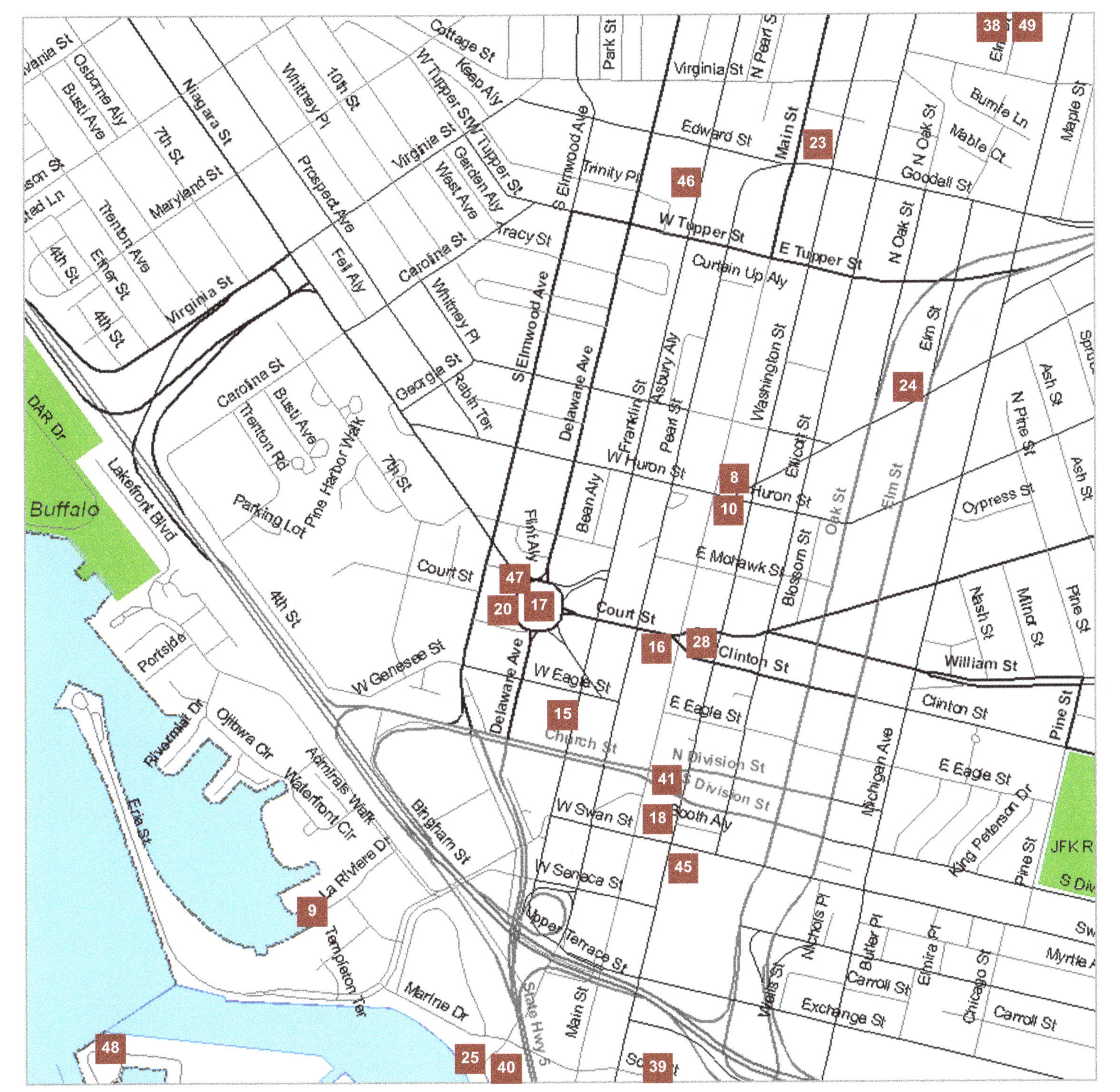

Cottage St
Park St
Virginia St
N Pearl S
38
49
Elm
Pennsylvania St
Osborne Aly
Busti Ave
7th St
Niagara St
10th St
Whitney Pl
W Tupper St
Keep Aly
W Tupper St
Virginia St
Garden Aly
West Ave
S Elmwood Ave
Main St
Edward St
Trinity Pl
N Oak St
Goodell St
Bumle Ln
Nable Ct
Maple St
23
46
dison St
sted Ln
Trenton Ave
Maryland St
4th St
Effner St
Prospect Ave
Fell Aly
Carolina St
Whitney Pl
Virginia St
4th St
Tracy St
W Tupper St
E Tupper St
N Oak St
Elm St
Carolina St
Georgia St
Rabin Ter
S Elmwood Ave
Delaware Ave
Curtain Up Aly
Washington St
Elm St
24
Trenton Rd
Busti Ave
7th St
Pine Harbor Walk
Parking Lot
W Franklin St
Asbury Aly
Pearl St
W Huron St
Ellicott St
Oak St
Ash St
N Pine St
Spru
DAR Dr
Lakefront Blvd
Huron St
8
10
E Mohawk St
Blossom St
Ash St
Cypress St
Buffalo
Flint Aly
Bean Aly
Court St
47
20
17
Court St
16
28
Clinton St
Nash St
Minor St
Pine St
Portside
4th St
W Genesee St
Delaware Ave
W Eagle St
Clinton St
William St
Riverview Dr
Ojibwa Cir
Waterfront Cir
W Eagle St
15
E Eagle St
Clinton St
E Eagle St
Pine St
Admirals Walk
Church St
N Division St
Michigan Ave
Erie St
Bingham St
41
S Division St
18
Booth Aly
King Peterson Dr
JFK R
La Riviere Dr
W Swan St
S Div
9
W Seneca St
45
Nichols Pl
Butler Pl
Elmira Pl
Sw
Myrtle A
Templeton Ter
Wells St
Carroll St
Chicago St
Marine Dr
Upper Terrace St
Exchange St
Carroll St
48
25
40
State Hwy 5
Main St
39
Seneca St

# About the author:

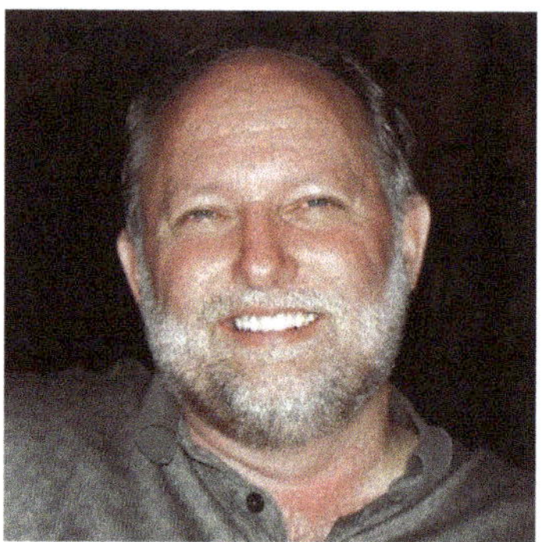

On the theory that history as an incomplete collection of facts is dull, tedious, and boring, Dr. Mark Donnelly, one of Buffalo's most boisterous civic cheerleaders, is at it again. Using his camera and slightly off-bubble sense of humor, he's unleashed his inner history wonk to tell the story behind the story and help everyone fall in love with the rich history that surrounds us.

Dr. Donnelly is an artist, an educator, a passionate community activist, a proud husband and father, and a man seldom separated from his camera. As one of the region's premier photographers, his work has appeared in dozens of exhibitions and galleries, including the Albright-Knox Art Gallery, Burchfield Penney Art Center, ZGM Fine Arts, Rodman Hall Arts Centre, and the Art Gallery of Hamilton.

Dr. Donnelly's most recent book, "Frozen Assets: The Beautiful Truth About Western New York's Fourth Season" is a whimsical look at Buffalo, New York's winter. Utilizing his Nikon and historical data from the National Weather Service, he views the city through the lens of perhaps our most misunderstood three months – our spectacular winters. You are invited to be inspired by the majesty of our city adorned in white, to debunk the exaggerations about our weather, and to laugh all the while you are doing it.

In his first book, "The Fine Art of Capturing Buffalo," he visually showcases Western New York's vast wealth of arts, heritage, and everything else that makes Buffalo an amazing place to live. It's a five-year body of his work, displaying his passion for the city, from the vast expanse of parks and gardens, architectural treasures, and our arts and cultural scene, to our proud past and positively brilliant future.

9 780984 878741